As Seen by Both Sides

★

The exhibition *As Seen by Both Sides* was curated by C. David Thomas and organized and circulated by the Indochina Arts Project. Lucy R. Lippard and David Kunzle selected the American work. The Vietnamese work was selected by David Kunzle, William Short, Lois Tarlow, and C. David Thomas, with the assistance of the Ministry of Culture in Hanoi and the Fine Arts associations in Hanoi and Ho Chi Minh City. All work from the United States is on loan from the artists. All work from Vietnam is on loan from the artists through the Fine Arts Department of the Ministry of Culture in Hanoi and the Fine Arts Association in Ho Chi Minh City.

Library of Congress Catalog Card Number 90–85140
Library of Congress Cataloging-in-Publication Data are available.
ISBN 0–87023–744–6
Distributed by The University of Massachusetts Press, P.O. Box 429, Amherst, MA 01004

As Seen by Both Sides is an original publication of the Indochina Arts Project of the William Joiner Foundation. For further information, contact Indochina Arts Project, 20 Webster Court, Newton Centre, MA 02159.

Edited by Debra Edelstein
Interviews copy-edited by Gloria Lee
Designed by Circle Graphics, Patricia Mullaly
Front cover: concept by Sumie Koike, photographs by William Short, design by Patricia Mullaly
Photographs of art and Vietnamese artists by William Short
Production Manager: Nancy Robins

Typeset in Janson by Graphics Express, Boston, MA
Color Transparencies by Color Services, Needham, MA
Printed by Dynagraf Inc., Boston, MA
Stock: Simpson Evergreen recycled paper and S.D. Warren Cameo
Bound by Bay State Bindery, Inc., Boston, MA

Photography credits: p. 40, Abe Frajndlich (detail); p. 56, William Short; p. 64, Lynn Hale (detail); p. 76, William Short; p. 90, Nina C. Olsen (detail); p. 94, William Short (detail); p. 98, Jim Reynolds; p. 110, David Crossley; p. 112, Cosimo Di Leo Ricatto (detail)

As Seen by Both Sides

American and Vietnamese Artists Look at the War

EDITED BY C. DAVID THOMAS

★

INDOCHINA ARTS PROJECT

AND THE WILLIAM JOINER FOUNDATION

BOSTON, MASSACHUSETTS

1991

DISTRIBUTED BY THE UNIVERSITY OF MASSACHUSETTS PRESS

CONTENTS

Preface 7

Foreword 8
Quach Van Phong

Foreword 10
Tran Viet Son

Acknowledgments 11

Introduction: Divided by War, United in Peace 13
C. David Thomas

Chronology 16

ESSAYS 19

The Meeting of Two Memories 20
Lucy R. Lippard

Two Different Wars 23
David Kunzle

EXHIBITION 33

INTERVIEWS WITH LOIS TARLOW 33

Nguyen Tho Tuong	34	Tran Te	74
Michael Aschenbrenner	36	Arnold Trachtman	76
Huynh Phuong Dong	38	Bui Tan Hung	78
Leon Golub	40	Quach Van Phong	80
John Plunkett	42	Nguyen Minh Dinh	82
Cliff Joseph	44	Benny Andrews	84
Tran Trung Tin	46	Tran Thanh Lam	86
Ngan Chai	48	Nguyen Tuan Khanh (Rung)	88
Nguyen The Minh	50	Richard J. Olsen	90
Nguyen Nghia Duyen	52	Le Tri Dung	92
Pham Nguyen Hung	54	William Short	94
C. David Thomas	56	Cynthia Norton	96
Tin Ly	58	Rudolf Baranik	98
James R. Cannata	60	Kate Collie	100
David Schirm	62	Rick Droz	102
May Stevens	64	Tran Viet Son	104
David Smith	66	Do Hien	106
Vu Giang Huong	68	Tran Khanh Chuong	108
Nguyen The Huu	70	Wendy V. Watriss	110
Trinh Kim Vinh	72	Nancy Spero	112

Checklist 114

Preview Opening:
Arvada Center for the Arts and Humanities
Arvada, Colorado
May 11–June 6, 1990

National Opening:
Boston University Art Gallery
Boston, Massachusetts
January 14–February 24, 1991

Wight Art Gallery, UCLA
Los Angeles, California
March 24–May 19, 1991

Art Center of Battle Creek
Battle Creek, Michigan
September 1–October 19, 1991

Waterworks Visual Arts Center
Salisbury, North Carolina
November 8–December 15, 1991

Art and Culture Center of Hollywood
Hollywood, Florida
January 9–February 16, 1992

The Baxter Gallery, Portland School of Art
Portland, Maine
March 16–May 3, 1992

Richard F. Brush Art Gallery
St. Lawrence University
Canton, New York
August 31–October 2, 1992

Lehigh University Art Galleries
Bethlehem, Pennsylvania
November 11–December 23, 1992

Atlanta College of Art Gallery
Atlanta, Georgia
January 21–March 10, 1993

Minnesota Museum of Art
St. Paul, Minnesota
June 15–August 15, 1993

Southwest Missouri State University
Southeast Asia–Ozark Project
Springfield, Missouri
November 1–December 15, 1993

National Museum of Fine Arts
Hanoi, Socialist Republic of Vietnam
1994

National Museum of Fine Arts
Ho Chi Minh City, Socialist Republic of Vietnam
1994

National Gallery of Vietnam
Hai Phong City
1994–95

National Gallery of Vietnam
Quang Ninh Province
1994–95

National Gallery of Vietnam
Vinh City
1994–95

National Gallery of Vietnam
Da Nang City
1994–95

National Gallery of Vietnam
Hau Giang Province
1994–95

The William Joiner Foundation is proud to present *As Seen by Both Sides*. As Quach Van Phong states in his foreword, the Vietnam War remains "a painful wound for the people of both countries." Through projects such as this, the Foundation seeks to help in the healing of these wounds, both in the United States and Vietnam.

David Thomas, William Short, Lois Tarlow, and the Advisory Board of the Indochina Arts Project are to be congratulated for their efforts here. It is our hope that this catalogue and exhibition will encourage many other artists, particularly veteran artists, to become similarly involved in the work of reconciliation.

In all its efforts, the William Joiner Foundation draws on the commitment of fellow veterans to promoting understanding of and healing from war. Veteran writers, artists, doctors, educators, nurses, counselors, printers, bankers, and people from diverse backgrounds and trades all play a vital part in the Foundation's work in areas of cultural, humanitarian, and educational development and exchange.

Since its establishment in 1988 the Foundation has sponsored exchanges between Vietnamese and American veteran artists, writers, physicians, and health workers; sent medical equipment to hospitals in Vietnam; and provided sewing machines, medicines, and prosthetics to centers for disabled veterans and their families. Through these activities, as well as efforts to help veterans and their families in the United States through support and advocacy for projects benefiting disadvantaged, homeless, and minority veterans, the Foundation seeks to create some positive legacy of the Vietnam War.

We thank you for your support.

The Board of the William Joiner Foundation

FOREWORD

Vietnamese artists love not only beauty but also their country and their people. They love freedom, peace, and happiness. In all their painting and sculpture, from ancient to modern times, there is an aesthetic ideal promoting peace, happiness, and a comfortable life.

But throughout its long history Vietnam has been plunged into war and subject to aggression, from slavery under Chinese feudalism to Japanese fascism, French colonialism, and finally the American war. The war between the United States and Vietnam lasted more than ten years and caused countless deaths and destruction from the country to the city, from mountainous regions to coastal zones—all over the long stretch of land from Lang Son province to Ca Mau province, which were plowed by bombs and shells. Each family, each Vietnamese has suffered loss. The physical, spiritual, and emotional damage inflicted on the land and its people has not only moved Vietnamese artists but also encouraged writers, journalists, film producers, painters, sculptors all over the world to create works decrying the war the United States waged against Vietnam. Among them we can find many American veterans, who, like Vietnamese artists, bear the heavy burden of war impressions.

Although the style, content, method of artistic expression, and angle of reflection of American and Vietnamese artists differ, the social significance of their work is the same. The American works indicate the artists' antiwar attitudes. They have opposed the bellicose forces who sent young Americans to die in foreign lands, have opposed the cruel destruction and slaughter inflicted by modern weapons, have described the tragic ending of Americans killed in action. They have asked for peace and reconciliation. Vietnamese artists from both the North and the South, from both the guerrilla base and the city, have expressed their emotions before the realities of a ravaged country and imprisoned, dying, murdered people. They have painted the deep griefs, the havoc, the death—but also praised the heroism, bravery, and sacrifice of Vietnamese soldiers, the solidarity between people and the armed forces, the firm endurance and the lofty sacrifice of the Vietnamese people throughout the war. Vietnamese painters have rarely resorted to symbolism or abstraction for their works about the war: the images they recall carry human content and allow them to express the innermost feelings, the great anguish, the generosity, and the optimism of the Vietnamese people.

The war is a painful wound for the people of both countries. The artists in this exhibition seek to heal that wound through mutual understanding, which they hope will lead to a sincere and long-lasting friendship between the two peoples. They know that though former enemies, they were all victims of a devastating war, they were the lovely sons and daughters of good mothers and fathers, they just were men and women caught in a conflict they did not always understand. And they know that they must struggle to heal the physical, spiritual, and emotional wounds of war, for the Vietnamese people, for the American people, and for mankind as well.

With good will and sincerity, people all over the world may come closer together in a universal civilization of human nature. The Vietnamese artists believe in this common cause and were very eager to participate in this exhibition, which will travel in both countries.

We offer best wishes for the ever-increasing and long-lasting friendship between the American and Vietnamese people!

Quach Van Phong
General Secretary, Fine Arts Association
Ho Chi Minh City

The art of Vietnam has a long and ancient tradition, whose origin dates to 300 BC. The Lac Viet people, believed to be the ancestors of the Vietnamese, left behind brass drums on which were engraved scenes of animal figures and portraits of the people's daily activities. Their craftsmanship reveals an art of great individuality and a bronze-casting technology that had reached a high degree of development. During the Ly and Tran dynasties (1010–1409) Buddhist arts matured, as shown in the architecture of temples and pagodas, in sculptures, and in wood and stone engravings. The art of this period, though influenced in part by the arts of China and India, maintained its distinct style and native flavor.

In addition, folk arts in the form of Tet (Lunar New Year) paintings, religious drawings, and wood engravings are distinguished by the simplicity of their colors, a sense of robustness, and a witty appearance. They provide a valuable heritage for our popular arts.

From 1884, when the country fell under French rule and the feudal system began to decline, the art of Vietnam was interrupted in its development for a long period. Not until 1925, when the French founded the Indochinese College of Arts, did Vietnam create its first crop of artists schooled in the European style of symbolic representation. Simultaneously, new techniques and materials were developed. Techniques such as lacquer and silk painting, which had been instrumental in creating the uniqueness of Vietnamese art in its past development, became powerful vehicles for contemporary expressions.

This exhibition of recent art about the United States–Vietnam conflict by artists from both countries will become a part of the history of Vietnamese art.

Tran Viet Son
President, Fine Arts Department
Ministry of Culture
Hanoi

ACKNOWLEDGMENTS

Organizing an exhibition of this scope is possible only through the efforts of many people. The lack of diplomatic relations between our two countries and the US trade embargo against Vietnam have made communicating and working with Vietnam especially difficult. The Vietnamese Foreign Ministry, and Foreign Minister Nguyen Co Thach, have given their full support to the project and been instrumental in granting permission for the exhibition. I would like to thank Nyugen Co Thach for his assistance, encouragement, and personal desire to ensure the exhibition's success. I would like to acknowledge the assistance of Tran Minh Dung, Third Secretary, Permanent Mission of the Socialist Republic of Vietnam at the United Nations, for making possible communication between our countries.

I would also like to express my gratitude to both Nguyen The Minh, former president of the Fine Arts Department of the Ministry of Culture, and its current president, Tran Viet Son, for their hard work in organizing the exhibition from their side of the Pacific, and to Vu Hung, former deputy director for International Cooperation for the Ministry of Culture, for his assistance and support. I offer thanks as well to Quach Van Phong, secretary general of the Fine Arts Association in Ho Chi Minh City, and Vu Giang Huong of the Fine Arts Association in Hanoi for their assistance and friendship, and to Executive Committee member Huynh Phuong Dong, for being who he is. The Swiss filmmaker Ho Quang Minh offered valuable assistance in Vietnam. A special thanks must be given to our talented interpreters in Hanoi, Lan and Chau.

Were it not for John McAuliff, director of the US/Indochina Reconciliation Project, this exhibition might never have been conceived. It was during his 1987 Educators' Trip that I met with Nguyen Van Chung, deputy director of the Fine Arts Museum in Hanoi, and began discussions about this exhibition. It was his early encouragement that gave me the determination to pursue the project.

I would like to thank Kevin Bowen and David Hunt, codirectors of the William Joiner Center, for their important contributions to the project's design, organization, and implementation. My thanks to Robert Glassman for providing the funds, the vision, and the leadership to begin the William Joiner Foundation and for having faith in the Indochina Arts Project. I would also-like to thank Bob and his wife Linda for opening their home for a most crucial fund-raiser.

I am indebted to the advisory board of the Indochina Arts Project, whose various talents have added greatly to the project: Tom Bird, Joan Lebold Cohen, Bill Ehrhart, Jock Reynolds, and Van Toi Vo. I am further indebted to assistant exhibition coordinator Bill Short and associate director Lois Tarlow. Bill's assistance with nearly every aspect of the exhibition, including two trips to Vietnam, has ensured its success. He has also photographed all the art and the Vietnamese artists for the catalogue. With determination and dedication, particularly under the difficult condition of working through interpreters in Vietnam, Lois interviewed all forty artists, enabling us to hear their stories in their own words.

Many thanks to our jurors, who have also contributed reflective essays to the catalogue. Lucy Lippard helped locate and select the American artists and continues to be an inspiration to artists of conscience. David Kunzle helped select both the American and Vietnamese work.

I offer thanks to Emmanuel College for providing both financial and moral support and to Sr. Janet Eisner, president; Dr. Helen M. Trimble, vice president for Academic Affairs; and other members of the faculty, especially those in the art department, for their encouragement.

I would like to thank the Arvada Center for the Arts and Humanities, Arvada, Colorado, for making the preview opening such a success. Thank you to curator Anne Soerensen, director of public relations Rita Lovato, and exhibition designer Charmain Schuh. The Arvada Center gratefully acknowledges financial support for this project from the Scientific and Cultural Facilities District, whose funds help make their programming more accessible to the citizens of metropolitan Denver.

Thank you to Boston University Art Gallery director Arlette Klaric and her staff for their support and work in hosting the national opening of the exhibition.

Support for the research and production of this catalogue and exhibition has been generously provided by Abigail Avery; *Art New England*; John and Charlotte Bemis; Bradford College; Color Services, Needham; Dickson Ticonderoga Co., Sandusky, Ohio; Emmanuel College, Boston; Hale & Dorr, Counsellors at Law, Boston; Hamill Studio, Boston; Ken-Kaye Crafts Co., Newton; Massachusetts Cultural Council, as administered by the Newton Arts Lottery, Newton; Massachusetts Cultural Council, as administered by the Cambridge Arts Council, Cambridge; The New England Foundation for the Arts, Boston; Rix Dunnington Superdrug, Auburndale; Shawmut Design Associates; University of Massachusetts, Boston; Vietnam Veterans of America Foundation; The William Joiner Center for the Study of War and Social Consequences, Boston; The William Joiner Foundation, Boston; the Washington Project for the Arts, Washington, DC. I wish to acknowledge as well the many individual donors who believe as we do that art can be used to heal wounds and teach us to see.

My very special thanks go to the talented team of people who have worked day and night to put this book together in only five months. Thanks to Nancy Robins, production manager; Debra Edelstein, editor; Patricia Mullaly, designer; and Gloria Lee, who copy-edited the interviews. I offer thanks as well to Jerry Roche, vice president of Dynagraf Inc., for his support and assistance with the printing.

A very warm and special thank you to my wife, Jean Thomas, for her professional skills as a fund-raiser and the many hours she has unselfishly donated. To my parents I can only say that I hope I am as able to give my children the ability to see an injustice and inability to turn away from it as they have given me.

My gratitude to the Bemis family—John, Charlotte, Ellie, and Jerry (Pugh)—for all their support and encouragement and for their continued efforts to make this a more kind, peaceful, and intelligent world.

A group of Vietnamese-American friends who, because of the political climate in the Vietnamese-American community, cannot be thanked by name have been a central part of the project since its inception. It was often your kindness, enthusiasm, and willingness to help, in spite of possible personal problems, that inspired me to continue.

Finally, the most important people to thank are the artists who, without hesitation, agreed to loan their work for more than four years. The artists of both countries have been extraordinarily generous in giving both their time for the interviews and their work for such a long period. It is nearly impossible for me to express my gratitude.

C. David Thomas
Director, Indochina Arts Project

March 22, 1970, was the happiest day of my life. After completing the 365th day of my "tour of duty" in Vietnam, I was headed back to "the world." For me the war was over, and, like thousands of other American veterans, I was ready to resume the life I had left behind. The American military presence in Vietnam was winding down after nearly ten years of involvement, and "peace with honor" was at hand.

That same year Madame Vu Giang Huong, professor of art at the College of Fine Arts in Hanoi, took her painting class on a field trip to the site of what had been, before it was destroyed by American aircraft, an important bridge linking Hanoi with its port city of Hai Phong. The students recorded the damage in their sketches and paintings and then returned later to assist the soldiers and local citizens in reconstructing the bridge. They also held exhibitions to raise the soldiers' morale. For them, the war of liberation that had begun against the French immediately after World War II, nearly twenty-five years earlier, was to continue for five more years.

By 1973 all American ground forces had left Vietnam and the southern effort was turned over to the Army of the Republic of Vietnam. The American people were relieved that the long ordeal was finally over for them and that calm was returning to American college campuses. I completed my undergraduate work that year and began graduate school.

Nguyen Tho Thong, one of the artists in this exhibition who currently lives in Hanoi, had joined the North Vietnamese Army the previous year at the age of nineteen. After a brief period in the infantry, he had returned to Hanoi to assist in the training of new soldiers.

On April 30, 1975, the last Americans departed from Vietnam, and the war we had fought for nearly ten years suddenly disappeared from American life. Only the presence of veterans and refugees reminded us of the human toll of that period. Many American veterans were having great difficulty adjusting to life at home. The Vietnamese refugee community was trying to adjust to life in America while looking back with bitterness and anger at the communists who had taken over their country. The US government broke diplomatic relations and imposed a trade embargo.

Madame Huong began another term at the School of Fine Arts, where she was named vice-director in 1977. Tho Thong, like most Vietnamese soldiers, stayed with his unit for the next seven years to begin rebuilding his war-ravaged country. His unit was assigned to rebuild the railroad connecting Hanoi with Saigon, now renamed Ho Chi Minh City.

The new government in Vietnam began the long process of healing the wounds of war and reconstructing the economy and country. Thirty years of war had left the population, economy, and landscape ravaged. During the ten years the United States had fought in Vietnam, the armed forces had dropped over 15 million tons of bombs (approximately 700 pounds for every man, woman, and child living in Vietnam) and sprayed 18 million gallons of poisonous chemical herbicides (nearly two quarts per person) over the forest and croplands of Vietnam.

In a country approximately the size of New Mexico and with a population of under 50 million, the Americans left behind 131,000 war widows, 200,000 prostitutes, and over 10 million refugees. While 58,135 American soldiers were killed, 1,921,000 Vietnamese died (over 60 percent of whom were women and children), and 300,000 orphans were created. The Vietnamese lack the resources to locate tens of thousands of their own people still missing from that war, yet through the trade embargo the United States continues to punish the Vietnamese for not locating the 1,678 (as of July 1990) Americans still listed as missing in action. (By comparison, after World War II 78,751 American soldiers were missing or unaccounted for, and the Korean War resulted in 8,177 MIAs.) Only recently has the US government given permission for the estimated 8,000 to 15,000 Amerasian children, now in their late teens and twenties, to emigrate to the States.

At the end of the war the Hanoi government found itself with an economy in the South which had been almost completely dependent on American aid for over ten years, a northern industrial base nearly destroyed by American bombing, and a southern agricultural economy in shambles from the defoliants, massive bombings, and flight of the farmers to the relative safety of the cities. The Vietnamese were forced to replace the economic void left by the American withdrawal with aid from the Soviet Union and China, as well as from Cuba, East Germany, and Poland, among others. More recently countries like Sweden, Australia, Japan, and France have offered assistance.

After 1975 the Hanoi government found its efforts to revive the country through a planned economy ineffective. The Sixth Party Congress in 1987 enacted sweeping economic reforms that rank with the great changes initiated by the socialist countries of Eastern Europe.

The task of rebuilding the country was made more difficult by the political instability in neighboring Cambodia, and in late 1979 Vietnam was forced to send troops into Cambodia to stop the genocide perpetrated under the Khmer Rouge leadership, which was spilling over into Vietnam. The criticism leveled at Vietnam for this act further isolated the country. Only recently have the conditions in Cambodia improved enough for the Vietnamese to feel they could safely withdraw their troops. The final chapter still remains to be written. The Khmer Rouge is still the major player in a coalition, whose primary supporters are the United States and China, attempting to overthrow the current government in Phnom Penh.

★ ★ ★ .

Americans had gleaned their knowledge of the war from television, where the nightly news showed the horror of American soldiers fighting and dying in the jungles of some mysterious country. In 1985 the war was back on the screen, in the form of a public television series entitled *Vietnam: A Television History*. Like other documentaries on the war, it concentrated primarily on the political and military aspects and on the problems in the States stemming from our involvement. As with the successful films to follow—such as *Platoon, Full Metal Jacket,* and *Born on the Fourth of July*—it offered only glimpses of the impact of the war on the Vietnamese. And these films all portray the Vietnamese as either inept soldiers from the south, vicious Viet Cong and North Vietnamese soldiers, or victims of a flawed American policy—but never as masters of their own destiny.

The numerous books by American veterans of the war vividly present the soldiers' experience, and books by historians, sociologists, and political scientists focus on American policy and the war's impact on American society. Only recently have we begun to hear Vietnamese voices on the subject: Le Ly Hayslip's sensitive and gripping *When Heaven and Earth Changed Places* was published in 1989, and a work by one of Vietnam's leading writers, Le Luu, is currently being translated into English and is expected to be released in 1991. *Thoi Xa Vang* will, for the first time, give Americans the opportunity to read about the war from the perspective of a former soldier of the North Vietnamese army.

Even the few art exhibitions on the subject have presented only the American viewpoint. The most notable are the multidisciplinary exhibition *War and Memory* organized in 1987 by the Washington Project for the Arts and the 1989 exhibition *A Different War: Vietnam in Art*, curated by Lucy Lippard and the brainchild of John Olbrantz at the Whatcom Museum of History and Art in Bellingham, Washington.

As Seen by Both Sides is the first exhibition to present the images and stories of artists from both countries. Through the art and interviews with the forty men and women who created it (twenty from each country), the people of the United States and Vietnam will finally have an opportunity to view each other's response to the conflict that changed so many lives. As the first major cultural exchange between our two countries since the war, the exhibition and accompanying catalogue may help rebuild our relationship and create a bond of respect and peace.

The few Americans, particularly veterans, who have been able to return to Vietnam have found the experience a healing one. In the process of designing and organizing this exhibition, I have traveled to Vietnam several times and have come to greatly respect the people I used to call my enemy and the one man I was told stood against everything I stood for, Ho Chi Minh. I have been warmly received by those who suffered and continue to suffer from the policies of my government. For those who are unable to travel to Vietnam, perhaps the exhibition and catalogue will spark an interest in the other side of the story, in the rich history and culture of Vietnam, in the people and what they were fighting for, and in the lives of Vietnamese people today. They have put the war behind them and are willing to teach us to do the same. It is time we accepted their challenge of "peace with honor."

C. David Thomas
Director, Indochina Arts Project

★

1858–83	The three historical regions of the 908-year-old kingdom of Vietnam—Annam (capital is Hue), Cochin China (capital is Saigon), and Tonkin (capital is Hanoi)—battle against French rule
1859	French capture Saigon and make Cochin China a French colony (1862–67)
1884	French declare protectorates over Tonkin and Annam
1887	Annam, Cochin China, and Tonkin are merged with Cambodia to form French Indochina
1942–45	World War II, during which the Japanese occupy the region
1945	After the Japanese withdraw, Ho Chi Minh, leading a coalition of nationalists and communists, forms his first government in Hanoi and declares Vietnam independent
1946	French attempts to reassert control and establish Bao Dai as emperor result in the First Indochina War
1954	After the defeat of the French at Dien Bien Phu, the Geneva Accords end the war and the region is temporarily divided into communist North Vietnam (incorporating Tonkin and part of Annam) and nationalist South Vietnam (incorporating Annam and Cochin China) pending nationwide free elections
1955	Fearing a communist victory, President Ngo Dinh Diem refuses to hold elections and declares South Vietnam an independent republic
	War of independence ensues as communist-led guerillas (the Viet Cong) try to overthrow the government of South Vietnam
	The United States sends military advisors to South Vietnam
1961	US sends support troops to South Vietnam
1962	The first defoliants, such as Agent Orange, arrive in Vietnam
1963	US troop strength at 15,000
	President Kennedy assassinated; Lyndon Johnson assumes office
	President Diem assassinated by South Vietnamese army after suppressing Buddhist dissidents
1964	After alleged clash between North Vietnamese gunboats and US destroyers in Gulf of Tonkin, President Johnson asks Congress for authority to retaliate and for mandate for future military action
	Congress overwhelmingly passes Tonkin Gulf Resolution supporting American efforts to "prevent further aggression"
	US bombs North Vietnamese PT boat bases
1965	Bombing of North and South Vietnam begins
	15,000 gather in Washington to protest bombings
	Nguyen Cao Ky becomes Premier of South Vietnam
	US troop strength at 184,300
1966	US troop strength at 385,300
1967	Nguyen Van Thieu becomes President of South Vietnam
	Antiwar rally in New York draws 100,000
	President Johnson raises US troop ceiling in Vietnam to 525,000
1968	"Tet Offensive" hands North Vietnam a major defeat
	President Johnson announces he will not seek reelection and halts bombing over North Vietnam
	Hanoi agrees to preliminary peace talks in Paris
	Richard M. Nixon elected President of the United States
1968–69	The height of the fighting:

American troops	543,000
South Vietnamese troops	819,200
Total allied troops	1,593,000
Communist forces	810,000
American air attacks	400,000/year
Bombs dropped	1,200,000 tons/year
Military defoliation	20,000 acres/year
Communists killed in action	200,00/year
Refugees	585,000/year
Civilian casualties	1,560,000/year

1969	President Ho Chi Minh dies
	Antiwar protests throughout the United States (250,000–300,000 protesters march on Washington)
	Reports of My Lai massacre by US troops
	President Nixon announces first US troop withdrawals
1970	US invades Cambodia
	Four students at Kent State University in Ohio are slain by National Guardsmen during demonstration against invasion of Cambodia
1971	US troop strength drops below 200,000
1972	US declares indefinite suspension of Paris peace talks
	Bombing of North Vietnam resumes
	Richard Nixon reelected
	US troop strength at 24,200
1973	President Nixon orders halt to US offensive air operations
	Peace pact signed in Paris by all parties and remaining US troops withdraw
	All US prisoners of war released
	2,500 Americans remain listed as missing in action (78,751 were unaccounted for at the end of WWII and 8,177 at the end of the Korean War)
1974	Both sides violate cease-fire agreement in South Vietnam
	President Nixon resigns; Gerald Ford assumes office
1975	Saigon falls to the North Vietnamese

At the end of the war:

Vietnamese dead	1,921,000
Cambodians dead	200,000
Laotians dead	100,000
Americans dead	58,135
Vietnamese MIA	200,000
American MIA	1,876
Indochinese wounded	3,200,000
Americans wounded	303,616
Vietnamese orphans	300,000
Vietnamese widows	131,000
Vietnamese prostitutes	200,000
Indochinese refugees	14,305,000

1975	Pol Pot's Khmer Rouge capture Cambodia and a reign of terror begins
1976	Jimmy Carter elected President of the United States
	North and South Vietnam officially unified as Socialist Republic of Vietnam
	US imposes trade embargo
1977	Normalization talks between US and Vietnam begin in Paris
	Khmer Rouge attack Vietnamese villages, killing hundreds of civilians
	Genocide by Khmer Rouge continues in Cambodia
1978	Secret negotiations for normalization between US and China begin in Peking
	Breakthrough achieved in unpublicized talks between US and Vietnam in New York
	President Carter shelves normalization with Hanoi in favor of closer ties with Peking
	US-China accord announced
	Vietnam invades Cambodia to oust the Pol Pot government
1979	Khmer Rouge driven from power by the Vietnamese
	China invades Vietnam to punish it for invasion of Cambodia; the attack is quickly repelled
	US trade embargo against Vietnam is extended to all forms of aid
1988	US and Vietnamese teams cooperate in locating the remains of missing American soldiers
1989	Vietnam withdraws all troops from Cambodia
1990	In October US and Vietnamese officials meet in Washington to discuss the continued US trade embargo, which the US links to the MIA issue and a satisfactory political settlement in Cambodia

ESSAYS

★

★

THE MEETING OF TWO MEMORIES

Lucy R. Lippard

Art, when it escapes from isolation as status symbol or lofty cultural artifact, can serve many more functions than our society has come to expect from it. In the case of this exhibition, art serves as a bridge across a space larger than oceans, and longer than the fifteen years since the closure of the "Vietnam era" (it was never officially a war). These images bring back memories of a time of anger. But if the anger has cooled, the horror cannot. No one knows better than the American and Vietnamese veterans that the scars of the war must remain visible in both countries so that we can avoid similar tragedies pending elsewhere in the world. As artists, these witnesses—direct and indirect—share that responsibility.

Those of us who protested the war from the United States, well-informed though we might have been about its evolution and progress and correct though we might have been about its immorality, never guessed at its substance. Of course the work in this show by American artists who are not veterans speaks movingly about their own experiences. But the heart of the Indochina Arts Project lies in the art by the veterans from both sides—and in what it means to us, now, that they have been brought together.

There is a certain humility and compassion in the work by the Vietnamese artists that is rarely found in American images of the war. (The exception is the work of a few veterans.) And there is a certain modesty to their work—partially determined perhaps by the paucity of materials and wealth in postwar, embargoed Vietnam. Given the warmth that David Thomas has found toward Americans in Vietnam today, it is tempting to relate that humility to a national comprehension of the long haul. Some of these artists may have been fighting for twenty-five years in a hundred-year war for liberation. Perhaps forgiveness is learned over time. Then again, perhaps the trauma has not yet been confronted. Nguyen The Huu told Lois Tarlow, "In Vietnam they hold exhibitions on many subjects and sometimes on a particular subject, but not on the activities of the war." Until recently, that was also true of the United States.

We know little of the context in which these Vietnamese works exist now, of the current Hanoi/Ho Chi Minh City "art world." We don't know the history, who influenced whom, what is traditional or derivative. So in order to come to this art with the pure (culturally unbiased) eyes it deserves, we must resist seeing everything in the context of our own art worlds, and our own imposed notion of what constitutes Quality. Because it is not, finally, so "foreign" either in style or content. Both "sides" reflect the common experience of men and women at war. (There are two Vietnamese women in the exhibition—Trinh Kim Vinh and Vu Giang Huong—but no American women veterans.)

20

The child is a recurrent symbol in art by both Americans and Vietnamese, which signals both a sentimental cliché and a moment of truth. It was the napalming of children—and the famous photograph by Nik Ut of the child Kim Phuc running, burning, naked down a road—that helped turn the tide of American public opinion against the war. Tran Khanh Chuong's triumphant child deity riding a blue horse over human cares is an image of hope and healing (no. 78), as is Le Tri Dung's grotesque child with umbilical cord floating as though reborn in the fiery orange sky above the shadows of battle (no. 59). Cliff Joseph's fat white baby plays with jewels and toys in front of the Statue of Liberty and the New York skyline, while a black baby broods without playthings, and cataclysm reigns in the "distance"—that is, Vietnam (no. 11). Benny Andrews's poignant portrait of an American soldier holding the body of a baby (no. 51), Rudolf Baranik's *Napalm Elegies* (nos. 65, 66), and David Thomas's Vietnamese child with barbed wire delicately etched across his face (no. 24) are echoed from a very different angle by Wendy Watriss's heart-rending images of the young American victims of Agent Orange (no. 80).

★ ★ ★

On the other side of the coin are the images of fighting men. The Vietnamese artists depict little combat and more of camaraderie and the day-to-day grind it takes to maintain a guerrilla war against the odds. They focus on their people and on the landscape they fought in and for. There are no Vietnamese counterparts for scenes like Richard Olsen's agonized helicopter pilot (no. 58), which expresses both empathy and "admiration for all warriors of all states" ("I felt like I was in the middle of the history of the world," he says), and Michael Aschenbrenner's terrifying evocations of combat memories painted on the walls of empty, dazzling rooms (nos. 3, 4). Contrast Aschenbrenner's nightmares with Tran Te's silk painting of a woman soldier arranging flowers in

a trench to celebrate Tet (no. 41), or with Nguyen The Minh's misty silk painting that transforms the advance toward battle into an almost joyous procession (no. 19), or Nguyen Tho Tuong's lovely evocation of a festival night, with people eating in a warmly lit hall while lovers embrace in the dark (no. 2).

Yet the Vietnamese artists have not forgotten the agony either. The bewildered, abstracted figures of Tran Trung Tin are set against a bleak gray sky and a church tower (no. 15). Nguyen Tho Tuong's mother, child, and young woman student, huddling in underground caves, are shielded from planes that scream overhead by a soldier whose arms extend across the painting in a protective cross form (no. 1). This may be the most precisely touching evocation of the Vietnamese experience in the show. In virtually every case, however, valor and hope prevail over fear. Do Hien's brilliantly colored collage (no. 76) celebrates victory with the "strong yellow to encourage the people to enjoy peace," as he told Lois Tarlow. Nguyen Tuan Khanh's sparkling expressionist figure of a woman holding candles (no. 55), lighting the way into the future, balances Nancy Spero's darker vision of a fleeing woman (no. 82). Underlying all of the culturally diverse art in this show is the shared experience of the anguish of patriotism and, sometimes, of the necessity to forego such loyalties in order to confirm a larger loyalty to humanity.

The intense paintings of Tin Ly, a Vietnamese who survived much of the war in Saigon before emigrating to the States, span the two sides. Both he and Jim Cannata recreate Eddie Adams's famous photograph of the Viet Cong suspect being shot by ARVN General Loan, another of the photographic icons of the era. For all its lurid coloring, Cannata's (no. 29) is a more reportorial view, while Tin Ly's two figures (no. 26) are separated by a stormy blue-gray, broken by what appears to be a beam of light shining down on the doomed man's head, as though the power of the gun were less than that of commitment to an ideal.

Tin Ly's work communicates one kind of double experience of the war. Bill Short's reveals another. A combat vet who came to resist the war in Vietnam, and was court-martialed for protesting, Short returned to Vietnam in 1989 and photographed his vet-artist colleagues there. He cracked and eroded the surfaces of his prints of people and places until they became metaphors for time passing and wounds not quite healed.

David Schirm's sympathetic paintings of the "enemy" as a family man, afraid of death, humanizes the "enemy" in a manner rarely found in the American art (nos. 30, 31). Rick Droz innovatively condemns the legacy of the war in his chilling juxtapositions of guns and prosthetic arms and legs (nos. 70, 71). David Smith's colorful, regimented battle ribbons, dotted with the ciphers of random fate (no. 34), and Kate Collie's austere still life of ribbons, bullets, pills (nos. 67-69) are moving understatements of the personal aftermath of international mayhem.

Cynthia Norton's ironic canonization of a bullet and her "altarpiece" centered on a beautiful waterfall and mountain landscape convey in very American style some of the solemnity of the Vietnamese work (nos. 63, 64).

Finally—and I hope I can say this without offending the individual artists—the show is more important than any single work in it. Not "just another group show," it is a masterpiece of internationalist cultural work, uniting the fragments of a multifaceted experience that changed (and took) the lives of so many. In the past decade this country has tried valiantly, if not always intelligently, to come to terms with Vietnam through the arts. But a piece was missing, a large piece. In *As Seen by Both Sides* we glimpse the shape of the Vietnamese memory—or the way the Vietnamese have chosen to remember. This can only alter our own remembering and, consequently, our own healing. ★

Two Different Wars

David Kunzle

"The War That Will Not End"[1]

"One day, Vietnam may become a country; for now, it remains a war, and a state of mind."[2]

There surely was never a single exhibition uniting art from two such divergent cultures. Can the yawning chasm of disparity in material wealth and political power, as well as in cultural and artistic traditions, be bridged by the sharing of one of the most destructive wars of modern history, when that sharing was so unequal? The sharing that counts now is different and posterior: the need for reconciliation.

These two—or forty or eighty-two—interpretations of one war prove a truism both psychological and political: that any reality, any history is the construct of cultural conditioning. Imagine, for a moment, the unimaginable: twenty American artists fighting in the conditions of the Vietnamese revolutionaries, and twenty Vietnamese artists fighting in the conditions of the Americans. Would the resulting art reflect the difference of the present conditions, or of the past conditioning?

It would be foolhardy to declare that the forty American works here are representative of the crazy-quilt of American art nationwide, or even of art about the war generally.[3] But they do reveal typical national tendencies toward the individual, personalist, eccentric, experimental, ambiguous, synecdochic, fragmented, abstruse, and contradictory—complexities that invite explanatory verbosities. Faced with such heterogeneity, can one even speak of an "American collective viewpoint"? As Lucy Lippard has said about the Vietnam War in general, there is no "master narrative."[4] The collective viewpoint of the Vietnamese, on the other hand, is comparatively traditional, homogeneous, cohesive, and direct. Apart from the difference in artistic traditions that have encouraged these different qualities in the respective countries, the art responds to a fundamental difference in attitude to the war.

Simply put, the war welcomed by neither group of soldier-artists was accepted by the one and repudiated by the other. For the United States, the war was fought over and through a tangle of contradictory purposes and political divisions; for the Vietnamese, the issues were relatively simple and illuminated by a broad national consensus. These differences mark the art as well as the conduct of the war.

The war in Vietnam, which on both sides propelled energies clear across the cultural spectrum—in song, theater, novel, and film—in the United States sharpened the anomie, existential guilt, and alienation on which the modernist tradition has thrived. To some Americans the war brought a political clarification; with others it exacerbated existing confusions. The antiwar movement pierced the rhetorical fog about American "rights" and "duty" to export "freedom" and "democracy," and it brought into focus the concept of "national self-determination" and the essential moral justice of any struggle to that end.

But while the war protesters agreed on the injustice of the American invasion of Vietnam, they were divided on the justice of Vietnamese armed resistance to it. The kind of pacifism that condemned our war and their war, this war and all wars without distinction, was as prevalent among artists (see interview with Benny Andrews) as among the population generally. So symbols from both sides of the war are jumbled in an indiscriminate negation (no. 57), and the deaths of Vietnamese women and children are deemed to "profit" the Vietnamese war effort (see interview with Cynthia Norton). Many American artists seem, vis-à-vis their Vietnamese counterparts, artistically overeducated and politically undereducated. The war, instead of enlightening, infantilized: "going to that war has made it very difficult for many of us to grow up."[5]

★ ★ ★

MILITARY LANDSCAPE

Psychologically and formally, ours is a culture of fragmentation. Vietnamese culture, paradoxically or logically, in the fire of the American (and other colonizing powers') onslaught upon it, fused into a cohesion and unity it had never known. This unity was facilitated by an economic system that does not give priority to individual initiative. While Vietnamese artists are encouraged to develop a personal style, a distinctive handwriting, they are not channelled by the demands of the market into strident eccentricities, as our artists are. Their art connects rather than separates. Vietnamese art is realistic, not as a result of the imposition of any concept of "socialist realism" but because of a shared and traditional perception of what constitutes artistic reality: the externally perceptible aspects of life and the land. Even, or especially, in the war-related subjects this exhibition

demanded, one senses a weaving into Vietnamese life as a whole, into the normal civilian economic and cultural fabric, and into the landscape which constitutes the permanent context.

While most of the Vietnamese art in the exhibition is more or less a portrait of the homeland, the history, countryside, and people of Vietnam as such are largely missing from the American art. Notable exceptions are the manipulated photographs of Bill Short and the drawings of David Thomas, which transcend the confusion and pain of the war underlying so many other pictures to bring into focus and humanize Vietnam itself. This process was facilitated by postwar visits to Vietnam in connection with the organization of this show, which is in itself a product of that necessary transcendence.

The absence of the Vietnamese, aside from their stereotypical roles as perpetrators and victims of terror, from American art and film relating to the war is not hard to explain in terms of political psychology. Unwilling to face the fact of defeat, Americans have refused to face the humanness of the victors, to recognize beauty in them and the land they inhabit. In David Schirm's *A Poem for All Wars* (no. 31) the substitution of a crazily scribbled wall (doodling from a personal unconscious, or American style wall-graffiti?) for the jungle setting his source suggested shifts the artistic priority to mental confusion: that generated in the participants individually, that of the war generally, or that inherent in the idea of guilt, capture, and death as coming at random.[6]

★ ★ ★

The sentimental attachment to the jungle landscape that is a constant in the Vietnamese art, on the other hand, was a motivating force in fighting the war. It was this homeland, these trees, these rice paddies that they were defending; and the continued viability of landscape as an artistic tradition (much attenuated in the West) parallels the traditionality of the Vietnamese struggle—two thousand years long!—to defend and wrest their land from foreign occupation. The recent wars in Vietnam are embedded in the deep, precipitous landscape of Vietnamese history.

Vietnamese landscape appears here in many different modes, but it is typically in harmony with the figures, naturalizing their activities, military and otherwise. The artists' sense of oneness between nature and people at war corresponds to the simple fact that the war was fought all over the country, penetrating deep into mountain and jungle areas that offered protection and refuge, in the classic and necessary manner of rural guerrilla warfare. The famous ability of the Vietnamese to merge into the landscape was the key to victory. In Tran Te's work the camouflage packs of the soldiers resemble the bushes, which are stylized into similar geometric patterns (nos. 41, 42). Art was made not only of this situation, but in and from it, for art classes and exhibitions were held in military camps, organized by artists (including some in this show) as part of or even superseding regular military duties. Art offered recreation and education, and built morale. Art was also created at the front, in times of battle, and on battle sites; Huynh Phuong Duong recounts how, in such circumstances, lacking proper brushes, he painted with twigs.

To this day the Vietnamese army cherishes and has institutionalized its role as patron of art, through exhibitions, prizes, purchases, and a special museum in Ho Chi Minh City called the Military Art Museum. In the environs of that city alone the political department of the army employs no less than twenty artists, all of them free to paint or sculpt whatever they choose. There is no obligation to depict the war, and there are no exhibitions specifically dedicated to it.

In Vietnamese art there is little or no killing and being killed. There is some firing of guns, there are a few pitched battles; but more typically we see the hauling of guns and the slogging of feet and heaving of equipment through the landscape. There is little bloodshed, and the wounded, when they appear, are the object of medical attention and acts of mercy. The traumatization of human bodies, through napalm and other horrors, that features so vividly in American films, photography, and posters, and here in the burnt figure paintings of Leon Golub (nos. 7, 8) and the *Napalm Elegies* of Rudolf Baranik (nos. 65, 66),[7] is transferred in the Vietnamese works to the lacerated landscape (nos. 5, 6, 50, 59, 60).

★ ★ ★

Other landscapes, by contrast, are poeticized. In Nguyen The Minh's silk painting (no. 19) foliage and figures melt into a vaporous acquiescence. Painting on silk, a favorite and traditional medium unfortunately underrepresented here, lends itself to effects that Western paint media cannot equal. Lacquer painting, another technique virtually unknown in the West, offers different possibilities, some of them quite "modernist" in appeal. Quach Van Phong (no. 48) manipulates his combination of paint, lacquer, and eggshell to evoke the particularity of a wartime jungle dwelling: the stone and log den built by the guerrillas in Ba Ra Mountain seems to offer a special protective crust grown by nature herself, on behalf of a prehistoric people still living in the closest intimacy with it. "Bomb them back into the Stone Age," indeed. Similarly Pham Nguyen Hung's *Soldiers Cooking at the Base Camp* (no. 23), with its expressive tufts of thatch and tree foliage merging with patches of shade, incorporates dwellings that are as natural and as permanent as need be; the Vietnamese can continue to fight from the jungle for another thousand years.

The other landscape by the same artist (no. 22) seems to me so tenderly expressive, so clearly transcendent of normal criteria of naturalism that I am tempted to interpret it through a Westerner's symbolic lens. A rickety-looking bamboo ladder follows the immense length of a slender tree, at the top of which a lookout is nested in dark thatch he seems to have flown in from elsewhere. The ladder in Western art has always been a symbol of human ambition; can Nature (or History), symbolized by the tree, offer sufficient support to such a hazardous quest? Neither tree nor ladders (there are two—the second even more precarious than the first) seem strong enough to bear a man's weight; but of such a delicately poised correlation of forces is revolution made. The handling has a Chinese delicacy and spontaneity of touch; the openness of form (the rest of the jungle is elided) conveys a palpable airiness.

As the guerrillas are naturalized elements of landscape, so their armaments are domesticated elements of costume. Peasant-soldiers bear the tools of war here, the tools of agriculture there, interchangeably. Western photojournalists have shown farmers quietly tilling their fields, with a rifle on their backs against the threat of some deadly American helicopter. And in the scenes of popular village and street life so well represented in Vietnamese art, though not here, the soldier is often barely distinguishable by his uniform and arms from the civilians.

★ ★ ★

In American culture, arguably the most militarist on earth, the soldiers are physically insulated from civilian society. Military bases are located outside the towns; ROTC may infest the UCLA gymnasium, but soldiers are seldom seen, in uniform, on the streets. Despite the power they wield in government (or perhaps just because of the inadmissible dimension of this power), the American military has never been accepted as a natural social factor, as traditionally in Europe. So that for American artists, soldiers appear as aliens, fearful and obtrusive. The monster-mercenary, a familiar figure in cartoons and satirical

posters, and the specialty of Leon Golub, has been confronted by few artists. Military and militarism appear in our show symbolically, fragmentarily, satirically, and covertly. In the religious icon of Cynthia Norton (no. 64) the bullet is transsubstantiated into sacrament, a thing divine; in Kate Collie's *Steve's Mementos* (no. 69) it is decontextualized and allegorically juxtaposed with other military symbols, old (decoration) and new (drugs). The gun is not worn, or borne, but exhibited as in a didactic museum installation, next to a prosthetic limb, a mutant of pathological evolution (no. 71). In a more realistic but still highly moralistic image, a cartridge belt is emblazoned across a soldier's back, an evil serpent-skeleton of bullets, independent of the witless khaki-camouflaged brain-pan above (no. 43). A more conventional, but exquisitely stylized, military stereotype is that of May Stevens's *Big Daddy Paper Doll* (no. 32), with his mindless paper cut-out patriotism—the smirking patriarch can slip on, interchangeably, the guise of Klansman/hangman, soldier, or butcher, all with toy bulldog.

There is one curious point of intersection in my polarization of the show into military naturalized and denaturalized: John Plunkett's vision (no. 9) of a landscape (this one palpably Vietnamese) in which guns lurk, disembodied in the bamboo, as if nature itself were armed against the intruder; the violence is "a feeling in the air, ready to erupt." The red ants, too (no. 10), seem to be an emblem of the enemy, pullulating everywhere, ready to bite, and die, rendered invincible by numbers and by the inhuman and superhuman strength of their social organization. The picture of the guns sprouting from trees also alludes to the primitive but effective ground booby traps laid by the Vietnamese. In reality they did not look like this, and the arrangement in the drawing looks like a diagram for a practical joke. (The version of a booby trap by Nguyen The Huu [no. 37] also has a whimsical quality.)

VICTIMS

If the American artists have tended to avoid the Vietnamese landscape, here as elsewhere,[8] how have they represented the Vietnamese people? Not as fighters, certainly not as victors (excepting perhaps Thomas's imperturbable Ho Chi Minh, no. 25), but as victims. The burnt, possibly napalmed flesh in Golub (nos. 7, 8), the child fraught with barbed wire (Thomas, no. 24), the mother fleeing with her infant (Spero, no. 81), the youth flashing the photograph of his family before the executioners (Schirm, nos. 30, 31)—these speak, as did so many comparable images from the war on television, on posters, and in art, to the guilt engendered by the spectacle of civilian suffering. The Pentagon propaganda which portrayed the "VC" as brutalizers of their own people paled before the mounting evidence of the effects of American bombing on the people at large, and the cold-blooded massacre of civilians such as that at My Lai.

The two most famous single photographs of the war—Nik Ut's photograph of the ten-year-old Kim Phuc fleeing, naked, screaming, her back burning with napalm, and Eddie Adams's photograph of the execution in a Saigon street of a VC suspect by the Saigon chief of police—have been incorporated into art countless times, the Adams picture twice in this small exhibit alone (nos. 26, 29). These "classic" images stand for random violence, one by fire from an invisible source at a very great height, destroying the obviously innocent; the other by fire from an un-bearably close and visible point, destroying the presumed guilty. But by the early 1970s, when pho-tographs such as these helped end the war, the idea and locus of guilt had dissipated in a fog of maniacally cultivated and usually falsified body counts. Either way, the guilt settles here, in the United States, like a radioactive dust of incalculable longevity.

The sense of the victimization of American soldiers, which eventually became quite intolerable to the American public, was fed from many sources. The pilot shot in his helicopter (no. 58) would be honored in the Vietnam Veterans Memorial in Washington, along with the many other casualties, who seem but few compared with the number who returned alive but proved irreparably damaged, psychologically as well as physically. Wendy Watriss's photographs (nos. 79, 80) are one small testimony to the pain and rage at the appalling suffering of survivors, responsi-bility for which was (is) denied by the Veteran's Administration, but with which the survivors and their families must live.

* * *

The Vietnamese tend not to talk of their dead, which they cannot count (they number in the millions),[9] to foreigners at any rate, or in their art. They have cemeteries, but no great, beautiful, gleam-ing, collective monument to their dead, as we do in Washington. Le Tri Dung's painting about the fetal deformity caused by Agent Orange (no. 59) is quite exceptional. The discretion which passes such horrors by is partly a matter of artistic tradition, which does not encourage the depiction of personal tragedy. During the war, such a picture would have been considered demoralizing. More remarkably, perhaps, the Vietnamese also tend to pass over the figure of the American aggressor, except in occasional renderings of the downed and captured pilot. He is treated as humiliated and sometimes faintly ridicu-lous, but nothing worse.[10] Posters and cartoons celebrate the extraordinary number of downed planes and pilots (shown with scowling, long-nosed faces), but it is the theme of the wounded American pilot tended by the Vietnamese nurse that appeals more to the fine artists. By this kind of presence, amid the absence of truly hostile representations of Americans, "the spirit of reconciliation," which is official policy and which strikes every visitor to Vietnam since the war, seems to have been internalized.

The potentially painful direct confrontation of the American pilot with the Vietnamese civilian imagined by Do Hien (no. 75) is distanced by the reduction of the American presence to helmet and flag, on which the woman and child seem to be meditating—as clues to the meaning or winning of the war, perhaps, or else just on the strangeness of its technology. If we factor in the soldier-artist's own account of how he watched the captured pilot die, observed the token of his love life, and honored his sacrifice as he would that of his Vietnamese comrades, the context becomes a meditation on death, love, and sacrifice itself.

Direct confrontation there is, but in very matter-of-fact terms that show the Vietnamese not so much as victors, but as teachers: Tran Viet Son's drawing of the prison officer explaining to a group of POWs the terms of their confinement (no. 72). This meeting across a table, with its commonplace air, like the same artist's views of prisoners standing and lying about, resting or sleeping, has a casualness that belies the long-lasting volatility of the situation depicted. Long after the stories of maltreatment and torture disappeared from the American press, fifteen years after the end of the fighting, allegations of the Vietnamese detention of POWs and failure to "account for" those missing in action are still used by the US government as motives for continuing its war on Vietnam by other means. The POW and MIA issue is still front-burner for the political right in the US, is still peddled by the media, is still capable of moving Air Force Intelligence to track me down and demand that I surrender all the data I had on Viet Son's drawings of POWs. In those sketches there is a listless air about the men, a boredom, a waiting for the resolution of their plight, for which they feel no responsibility; I was not surprised to hear from the artist, who talked to the prisoners himself, that they seemed unrepentant. The boots in the lower left corner of no. 73 (and there are separate sheets by the same artist with boots seen from all angles and with peculiar precision, as if they struck the sandal-shod Vietnamese as

a new kind of military fauna) seem to have more psychological definition than the prisoners.

★ ★ ★

A MODERNIST AND LIBERAL "SOCIALIST REALISM"? This is not the place for some definition of socialist realism, or a decision about how far this term fits the art, which is certainly realist, of Vietnam, which is certainly socialist. It is enough to contrast the variety of styles manifested in this exhibition, in the art I saw in Vietnam, and in the published art literature of the country,[11] with the relative homogeneity of styles, safely classifiable as socialist realist, displayed in a large collection of Chinese art in support of the Vietnamese.[12] Such stridency of tone, as well as the (to us) rhetorical cheerfulness and occasional grimness, are not characteristics of Vietnamese art, which is quieter and more relaxed, even when we consider the "patriotic" scenes in isolation. While the art is predominantly realist, it is often varied by modernist elements, but not in the self-conscious emulation of the West one finds in the socialist countries of Eastern Europe and in China of recent years, where modernism has had to do battle with an officially entrenched socialist realism.

The modernist elements in Vietnamese art may be viewed, in part, as reinforcement and variation of the geometric and abstract tendencies already inherent in native and Chinese-derived stylizations, which are particularly apparent in the treatment of the human form. These rarely reach complete nonfigurative abstraction, which is experienced as "strange" (as one art professor put it to me), although it certainly is practiced. The two works by Nguyen Tuan Khanh in this show (nos. 55, 56) are, I suspect, close to the edge of acceptability, and appear here perhaps as a gesture toward Western taste; this artist, a southerner and ex-ARVN (South Vietnamese army) officer, was heavily imbued with American culture. The child-like, clumsy look of the work of Nguyen Tho Tuong (nos. 81, 82) and Tran Trung Tin (nos. 13-16) is also not typical.

Careful craftsmanship, coupled with apparent freedom and spontaneity of touch, which is the essential dialectic of the Chinese tradition, is much in evidence; and stylization transcending anatomy, especially of the female form, tends to enhance the soft and supple, to evoke purity and tranquillity.

Modernist European and American art reaches the Vietnamese largely through reproductions, limited in number and often of poor quality. The library of the School of Fine Arts in Hanoi contains no more than a few dozen volumes, many of them of Soviet origin. A small number of Vietnamese artists have won scholarships to study abroad, mostly in Eastern Europe and the Soviet Union, none in China or Japan. Modernism took root mainly through the French tradition, which dominated education through World War II, and lingers; but all art professors at the moment are Vietnamese, most of them trained in Vietnam. The various kinds of assistance Vietnam has received from abroad, which has broadened considerably since the end of the American war, have been of a technical rather than cultural or artistic kind. To be sure, an improved economy comes first; cultural progress will follow.

★ ★ ★

The Vietnamese Fine Arts Association has relations with fourteen countries, mostly socialist, but only with Cuba and Mexico in the West. Rene Mederos, a Cuban artist with a very commanding style, arrived in Vietnam in 1969–70 to make a beautiful series of silk-screen prints about the struggle[13] and taught some classes in silk screen, then new to Vietnam. There are some Vietnamese posters remarkably Cuban in style; the country's poster art, borrowing rhetorical techniques which capitalism has fine-tuned, has proven consistently receptive to Western

modernism, especially Art Deco.[14] Cubans may have built the best luxury hotel in Hanoi (the Victoria) and improved the health of people and livestock (see no. 17), but they have left no comparable artistic legacy.

Nor have the Soviets. The most prestigious product of the Soviet-Vietnamese alliance was the space-flight program commemorated in posters and on a 1983 set of postage stamps. The chief monument to the Soviet public art style, apart from some architecture, is the colossal statue of Lenin donated by the Soviets and standing in Lenin Park in central Hanoi, which is the butt of unflattering jokes by the Vietnamese. The rhetorical blast of Sino-Soviet socialist realism must have threatened, for a moment, to carry off Vietnamese monumental sculpture (which in practice is eclectic rather than Soviet in style), to judge by some grim plaster pieces in the courtyard of the School of Fine Arts in Hanoi. When I asked why, if professors and students disliked them so much, they were allowed to remain, I got the pungent reply "as a warning." (The reaction of Nicaraguans to what they called "The Incredible Hulk" in Plaza Revolucion, Managua, was similar.) The only things Russian in our exhibition (discounting the originals of the armaments depicted) are the scraps of yellow paper with Russian texts oddly collaged into Do Hien's *Anniversary of the National Defense War* (no. 76).[15] The principal figures in this design, which has a monumental quality, relate more to the tradition of Vietnamese popular imagery than to any foreign model.

If the styles of Vietnamese art do not lend themselves to fruitful analysis in terms of socialist realism, how do the themes respond to the assumption that socialist systems give priority to overtly patriotic subject matter? The results here are surprising, and confirm the insight I gained from the initial resistance of the Vietnamese officials to the very concept on which this exhibition is based: that the art should focus on military experience. Such resistance was partly due, to be sure, to a diplomatic sense that the first exhibition of contemporary Vietnamese art in the United States, designed to heal the breach between the two countries, should not remind Americans of the war they lost, and that they should want to forget. But there is more to it.

"Patriotic" subject matter has never been more than a small part, if an inevitably privileged part, of artistic production in Vietnam. In the mass of prints, drawings, and paintings made on speculation for the open market, and lying in huge, amazing, indiscriminate piles on tables in the thirty or so arts and crafts galleries of Hanoi, patriotic subject matter has very little place at all. The vast majority of works are landscape, still life, and genre scenes, with a (perhaps) surprising quantity of mildly erotic female nudes (sentimental eroticism also flourishes in advertising and commercial iconography). At the other end of the market, the elite art collected in museums and books, which present to the the world the "public face" of the country, might be expected to tilt in favor of "socialist" or patriotic (military, political, historical) subjects.

Yet in two representative surveys of Vietnamese art, *Vietnamese Contemporary Painters* of 1987, with 156 works reproduced, and the big, luxurious picture book printed in Hungary in 1975, with 124 subjects reproduced,[16] the proportion of "patriotic" subjects is about one-fifth. In the latter book, which covers all media and was prepared before the end of the war (1973, the date of the preface), many of the subjects I count as "patriotic" are really landscapes using small military figures as staffage. About another fifth of the works reproduced are pure landscape, and yet another fifth are landscapes with some kind of agricultural activity that is more or less prominent, but not conceived in the propagandist-heroic manner of Soviet or Chinese socialist realism. Another fifth of the subjects show small-scale industrial or artisanal production, again not in a heroic or romanticized

way. The proportion of overtly patriotic subjects in three collections of *Sang Tac My Thuat* art magazine, each with over a hundred reproductions, is not very different,[17] nor is that in a portfolio of lacquer paintings.[18]

War and revolution is just one theme among many. The relative paucity at the elite level of nudes, still lives, portraits of individuals, and certain other traditionally popular subjects should alert us to the "socialist" preference for social life: village and street, social types, folklore, workers at work—all of which are, in the extended sense, patriotic: they all celebrate, poetically and prosaically, Vietnamese life. An editorial note appended (in English) to *Sang Tac My Thuat* magazine for 1979 expressed the idea of "patriotic extension" thus: "Parallel with works illustrating Socialism, construction and national defence, the portraits, landscapes, still lifes contribute greatly to the rather profound expression of the heroic Vietnam and Vietnamese." What is excluded here is the kind of inward exploration of the individual psyche characteristic of Western modernism.

★ ★ ★

A broad, liberal interpretation of "socialist realism" is also manifest in literature, to judge from the translated anthology *Vietnamese Literature*.[19] By Western standards this, like the publicly available art, is limited in thematic scope. Skeptics will of course look for signs of censorship, which was certainly imposed some months after the liberation of the South: "In September 1975, the Ministry of Information and Culture banned 56 of the roughly 1,000 authors (in the south) and over 200 of the thousands of books in circulation at that time." Since in 1973 only 20 percent of such books were Vietnamese originals, one wonders how many foreign titles fell under this ban. The main target was, presumably, indigenous "reactionary" literature, the taste for which was not and could not be wiped out quickly, after so many years of a "mongrel [US-supported] regime," which had "soiled the minds of our young people."[20] The repressive period of the late 1970s in the South, which coincided with a rigidly imposed "command economy" and "forced equalization," now recognized as a mistake, gave way in the 1980s to some liberalization, although the rhetoric of the need to "build socialism through culture" continues.

In the North, the Fine Arts Association, in a preface to a book of Vietnamese art published in the Soviet Union in 1959,[21] refers to a "struggle to separate art and politics" that was defeated in 1956–57. It is not clear how serious this was, but certainly no censorship and artistic repression on the scale suffered in China during the "Cultural Revolution," or in the United States during the McCarthy era, happened anywhere in Vietnam. Over the last decade the occasional articles with theoretical titles such as "Establishing a Socialist Culture," "Aesthetic Character of Socialist Realism," "Striving for Vietnamese Socialist Plastic Art,"[22] reflect official concerns, no doubt, but do not seem to determine production; nor did the artists we spoke to seem particularly concerned to produce a "socialist" art. Their ambition, like ours, is simply to produce "good" art. ★

1. Title of an article by Jonathan Mirsky, *New York Review of Books*, August 16, 1990, p. 29, which reviews eight recent books on Vietnam.

2. "Khmer Ruse," editorial, *The Nation*, August 13/20, 1990, p. 152.

3. This is the subject of a superlative selection and analytic narrative by Lucy Lippard, *A Different War: Vietnam in Art* (Bellingham, WA: Whatcom Museum of History and Art, and Seattle: Real Comet Press, 1990).

4. Lippard, p. 115.

5. Schirm, cited in Lippard, p. 82, and interview with David Smith included here.

6. From a private conversation with the artist, I learned that the pictures illustrated an incident in which a Vietnamese caught in the jungle by an American patrol flashed at his would-be murderers a photograph of his wife and family, in an effort to save his life. The white silhouette figure is that of a guardian angel.

7. See also Lippard, pp. 28 and 46.

8. In Lippard we find perhaps two Vietnamese landscapes (pp. 46 and 47) among a few American landscapes rendered symbolically and satirically.

9. "[The North Vietnamese] accept[ed] one of the greatest losses of life in wartime, in relation to population, of any modern country." According to Dean Rusk, "their total casualties throughout the war were roughly equivalent to ten million American casualties" (Mirsky, pp. 29, 30).

10. The example best publicized in Vietnam is the woman artist Dang Thi Khue's *American Pilot Taken Prisoner*, a somewhat cubist-influenced oil of 1980, in which the pilot's head appears wittily over the rump of the ox drawing the cart he sits in (reproduced in *Vietnamese Contemporary Painters* [Hanoi: Red River Foreign Languages Publishing House, 1987], p. 148).

11. This is scant, mostly in Vietnamese, which I do not read or speak, and was not fully available in the Hanoi National Library when I visited.

12. *The People of Vietnam will triumph! The U.S. Agressors will be defeated!—A Collection of Chinese Art Works in Support of the Vietnamese People's Struggle* (Peking: Foreign Languages Press, 1966). None of the roughly 125 works reproduced is credited to an individual artist. I have seen no Vietnamese art publication that fails to do this.

13. Exhibited at the UCLA venue of this exhibition.

14. See the collection *Tranh Co Dong* (Hanoi: Nha xuat ban van hoa, 1977). The poster most strikingly Cuban in style, a portrait of Ho Chi Minh by Viet Quang (1972), appears in first place, as it were a frontispiece of the book. Another example of Cuban influence is the Vietnam-Cuba solidarity poster of 1968 (pl. 24). Mederos's Vietnam series is featured in *My Thuat Tap Chi Cua* 4:7 (1981), p. 91.

15. I doubt that the artist could read them, but one of these scraps refers to Vladimir Visotsky, a very popular Russian singer and writer who was banned under Brezhnev, committed suicide in 1972, and is now a hero of the progressive movement.

16. *Nghe thuat tao hinh Viet Nam* (Hanoi: Nha xuat ban van hoa, 1975).

17. (Hanoi: Nha xuat ban van hoa, 1977, 1978, and 1980).

18. *Lacquer Paintings of Viet Nam (A Selection of 40 Lacquer Paintings 1945–75)* (Hanoi: Foreign Languages Press, 1977).

19. Edited by Nguyen Khac Vien and Huu Ngoc (Hanoi: Red River Foreign Languages Publishing House, n.d.), recast from *Anthologie de la Litterature Vietnamienne*, 4 vols., 2,200 pp.

20. *Vietnamese Studies*, "Cultural Problems," 52 (1978), pp. 11, 44.

21. *Vietnamese Art* (Sovietsky Chudoznik, 1959). The book, with text in four languages, was based on the first exhibition of Vietnamese art, held in Moscow in 1958.

22. *My Thuat Tap Chi Cua Hoi My Thuat Vietnam* (Review of the Vietnamese Fine Arts Association), 1981, 1986.

EXHIBITION

INTERVIEWS

WITH LOIS TARLOW

★

NGUYEN THO TUONG

Although Nguyen Tho Tuong was enthusiastic about painting as a young boy, he had received no formal art training when, at the age of nineteen, he joined the North Vietnamese army. He worked in the propaganda section and assisted in the training of new soldiers before they went into battle. Like many of his colleagues, he got his first art training in the army, where he took a six-month course in painting in which he was taught to make posters and on-site drawings of military activities.

LT What was your job after the liberation in 1975?

NTT My unit rebuilt the railway linking the North to the South. Many sections had been destroyed. We also made new sections. When I left the army in 1982 I went to study at the School of Fine Arts in Hanoi. There I was trained in painting, sculpture, and printmaking and helped to develop further my drawing. It was a good time to use my life experience and to make interpretations of what I had seen.

LT Were there other students like you from the military in art school?

NTT Many, many. Most artists, because of the war, did not have conditions favorable to completing their fine-art training. After the war, many returned to finish their courses.

LT Let's talk about the extraordinary painting *Eyes of the War*. It has a lyrical quality of both tragedy and hope.

NTT I have a very deep impression and recollection of the people who were living under the raids of the B-52 bombers. I know the hardships. In spite of them, people like this woman in my painting are studying for the future. Here is the symbol of the mother taking care of her child under the explosions of the bombs. Her rifle is ready for combat. The man's symbol is the soldier of the National Liberation Front in his blue uniform. In my opinion, this fighter is a symbol, like a god, who safeguards the people from attack.

LT The soldier looks very protective of the whole environment and almost like a crucifix. The whole village seems to be supported on his outstretched arms.

NTT That's right. Also, he holds a rifle and a hand grenade.

LT The style of the painting is very different from any of the other work we have seen. Your use of color, line, and light and shade is unusual. It is fascinating how the figures also form the eyes.

NTT This is a picture with many meanings. One of the eyes is blind because there is no more significance to the fighter.

I have a very deep impression and recollection of the people who were living under the raids of the B-52 bombers. I know the hardships. In spite of them, people like this woman in my painting are studying for the future.

1. EYES OF THE WAR, *1989, mixed media on paper, 11 1/4 x 15 1/2 inches*

2. THUYEN QUANG CAFÉ, *1987,*
pastel on paper, 12 1/2 x 12 3/4 inches

MICHAEL ASCHENBRENNER

As Michael Aschenbrenner landed in Vietnam, the Marines called an air strike. Jets dropped two 500-pound bombs, killing fifteen Americans. "It was a rude awakening for an eighteen-year-old kid," he later remarked. Aschenbrenner was reassigned, as one of the replacements for the casualties, to a base camp at Phu Bai, from which he went out to live in the jungle for the next six months. His job was to inform the bombers and helicopter gunships where an attack was needed.

"In the first week, I realized we were not there to win a war or to help the children who were starving and raiding our garbage. I told the lieutenant, as I got assigned to this reconnaissance platoon, that I objected to the whole thing. He said, 'You'll go to Long Binh Jail.' I couldn't have done a search-and-destroy mission, but there were people in my unit who amply made up for my objections. The war in Vietnam had a way of making boys bloodthirsty."

Like many returning vets, Aschenbrenner just wanted to forget the war. At first he was unaware that the war had insinuated itself into his work. In 1969, when he was in a hospital being treated for leg injuries, he met Richard Harris, who had had three inches of his femur shot out and his sciatic nerve severed. He chose amputation over a lifetime in a brace. The two men became good friends and in occupational therapy together learned to scuba dive. It was through the friendship that the war entered Aschenbrenner's art.

"Richard Harris became my alter ego. I could say things in my art about him that I was truly saying about myself. For me, art shouldn't be about personal problems or neuroses. It should be more universal."

Aschenbrenner says it took him about ten years "to comprehend what happened to me in Vietnam and to start doing Vietnam-related images." Now all his work, with the exception of some pottery that he does not exhibit, explores his experience of the war. The *In My Room* series, whose title derives from a Beach Boys song, evolved from "a trying and tearful time alone in my room confronting my fears." After Vietnam, the artist says, "that's all I had."

Ernest Hemingway said that it took ten years after the First World War was over before he could write about it. I understand this. It has taken me as much time to comprehend what happened to me in Vietnam and to start doing Vietnam-related images.

3. In My Room Series: I, *1986–87,*
watercolor and colored pencil on paper, 22 x 28 inches

4. In My Room Series: II, *1986–87,*
watercolor and colored pencil on paper, 24 x 17 7/8 inches

HUYNH PHUONG DONG

Someday, when this country can see beyond the war, there will be a Vietnamese ambassador to the United States. Huynh Phuong Dong would be the perfect choice. He is wise, warm, full of life, and a very funny raconteur. Although one of the older artists in the exhibition, he is one of the youngest in spirit. He told us that he shaves two years off his age so that he can work longer and goes by the name of his son. His true name is Huynh Kon Nya.

LT Did you go to art school?

HPD Yes, from 1941 to 1945 I went to the School of Practical Art in Saigon. It's a famous art school. After that, I was a soldier for nine years and fought against the French. Then I studied at the School of Fine Arts in Hanoi for six years. In 1963 I came back to fight in the South. Now I just paint all the time at home in my private studio.

LT Were there differences between being an army artist in the French and American wars?

I met some American prisoners. Some of them shed tears. They never wanted the war. I understood that they did not know the reason for it. I felt sorry for them. I did some paintings and drawings of them.

HPD My paintings show big differences. In a minute the American bombs made forests into deserts. Agent Orange and napalm caused great destruction. You can see it in this painting, *The Bloody Battle of the American Battalion at Binh Gia*. I made it right after the fighting, because I might die and have no chance. I painted directly from the tube and chewed twigs to make brushes. The battle in the other painting, *Tombs of American Soldiers at Tay Ninh Battle*, took place near the barracks, so I painted it as it happened. I did this larger version at home later.

LT You have captured with much simplicity the bleakness of battle: the broken trees, the ammunition lying around, and the tanks, which were the tombs. The composition is a very dynamic force in communicating the aftermath of battle. Did you ever meet any Americans?

HPD I met some American prisoners. Some of them shed tears. They never wanted the war. I understood that they did not know the reason for it. I felt sorry for them. I did some paintings and drawings of them.

LT You and American artist Bill Short have become good friends. You were both in Ben Kat on different sides.

HPD When I went with Bill to Ben Kat, I knew he wanted to pass through and away from the old feelings he had when he was a soldier. He is a friend with whom I can share talks about everything, about culture, about art.

5. TOMBS OF AMERICAN SOLDIERS AT TAY NINH BATTLE, *1967, gouache on paper, 29 1/2 x 71 inches*

6. BLOODY BATTLE OF THE AMERICAN BATTALION AT BINH GIA, *1965,*
watercolor on paper, 13 x 18 1/2 inches

LEON GOLUB

Leon Golub is a gentle and humorous man whose paintings are brutal exposés of injustice and the abuse of power. It was inevitable that he would take up the war in Vietnam as well as the conflict in El Salvador. When art in America was cool, remote, and minimal, Golub's paintings about predation and the primitive, base nature of the human race were largely ignored. In the last few years the art world has caught up with him, and his exposés of unsettling realities are internationally applauded.

LT How did you come to deal with such horrifying subjects?

LG When my wife, Nancy Spero, and I lived in France, the Algerian War was going on. As Americans, we were aware of it, but considered it a French problem. We returned to the United States when the Vietnam War was going on. That was an American problem, and we became acutely aware of it. I joined the Artists' and Writers' Protest against the war and took part in many of its activities.

LT What were your paintings like at that time?

The war got into my work...through a long-standing interest in ancient and primitive art. I was looking for something raw and irregular with residual, implacable, human emotions. I wanted these emotions to be highly eroded and worn down.

LG I was doing large paintings based on Greek sculpture of male nudes struggling with each other. I was very interested in tension, hostility, and struggle. I soon became conscious of the gap between what I was doing and what was happening in the world. But it was hard for me to cross the gap because I felt there was an existential base to these generalized figures.

In 1969 I took some paint that I had scraped off the canvas, mixed it with black and red, and, with a sculpture tool, smeared it on a figure. It resembled napalm. It was the beginning of the *Napalm Series*. I did five large paintings. I was getting close but not close enough.

LT The silk screen in the show is from this period.

LG It took a couple of years before I did the first Vietnam paintings where the figures actually wore uniforms. The first one was still rather vague, with one figure bare chested and the other wearing blackish pants. The next one, however, had an armored car, GI issue, wrinkles in the clothes, and lots of details. I had crossed the gap by moving from the general to the photorealistic.

So, the war got into my work in a current way but through a long-standing interest in ancient and primitive art. I was looking for something raw and irregular with residual, implacable, human emotions. I wanted these emotions to be highly eroded and worn down.

40

7. NAPALMED HEAD, *1969,*
acrylic on canvas mounted on wood, 13 x 13 inches

8. THE BURNT MAN, *1970, silk screen on rag paper, 34 x 46 inches*

JOHN PLUNKETT

John Plunkett served in the infantry in the rubber plantations near Ben Kat and Tay Ninh. His combat experience, he says, consisted of "waiting with bait in the woods for someone to happen by. I sometimes felt like I was participating in a murder." He understood that "of course they did the same thing, but it was their country." Like many artists who did tours of duty in Vietnam, Plunkett took up that experience in his work many years after his return.

JP I didn't have an inkling that the subject was going to come up. I go through periods with my work when I'm in a sort of wasteland. I have no plan. I just start drawing. What took over were images of Vietnam. I suppose it's my own difficulty in understanding violence and my witnessing and participating in these acts that has driven me to make these pieces.

Violence is not always loud. It is sometimes quiet and quick. Sometimes it's a feeling in the air, ready to erupt.

LT These two drawings have an eerie menace. They are very beautiful and spare, saying only what's necessary. They have an oriental feeling. Is that intentional?

JP No, actually they are the crudest of anything I've done.

LT Besides these drawings, are you doing paintings of the war?

JP I started doing paintings of claymore mines, but at first they didn't turn out. They seemed too contrived. Once I eliminated the human body, they worked. I have a lot of new pieces that are smaller and much more violent. I paint them on wood panels with paint left over from my nonviolent work, which is much more passive, more about paint. Circles, squares, triangles, and space are the whole subject. I'll show you some fairly recent work about the war.

LT What are these images?

JP Bullet holes, and these are body bags and sharks.

LT That's terrifying. Why sharks?

JP Sharks have a singlemindedness to consume, and they make you think of violence and dismemberment. Artists have always been drawn to inhuman acts. No matter how civilized man becomes, he's never far from the beast.

9. Ambush behind Thin Woodline, *1988,*
graphite on canvas, 40 x 54 inches

10. Meeting Red Ants in Bamboo, *1988,*
graphite on canvas, 40 x 54 inches

★

CLIFF JOSEPH

Everything Cliff Joseph paints grows out of his deep concern for the state of the world, be it the possibility of nuclear war, the destruction of the environment, or the abuses wrought by apartheid. It was natural that during the Vietnam War Joseph's paintings would reflect his deep opposition.

LT You had your own commercial art studio. Why did you give it up?

CJ I started becoming political. Being a commercial artist and a serious social commentator didn't work for me. That's when I got into painting.

LT *The Playpen* and *Isaiah II:4* are very disturbing. When did you start doing paintings in response to the Vietnam War?

CJ During the protests. I also joined marches and demonstrations. These pieces are inspired by the war in Vietnam, but they speak about war in general.

LT Do you still do work from the war?

CJ No, I made my statement. Now I fear we're leading up to a nuclear confrontation by just having this force around when there are such hotheads in the Middle East. We must work to head it off. More people must get involved. The government keeps us focused on symptoms when we need to deal, before it's too late, with the causes of violence—why people use crack, why they mug and kill each other, set fires, rape women.

LT It does feel like a large portion of humanity is on a self-destructive course.

CJ Yes, very much so. I feel personally that I should be involved in trying to find solutions to these problems. But I also feel that this is an undertaking for all artists. I believe there should be an international organization of artists, writers, and performers for these global problems. It must be a continuous, consistent effort.

LT What have you focused on in your recent work?

CJ Last year I did a painting of a young South African woman. People see her beauty and her rose before they see her gun. She is saying to the apartheid regime, "You can choose my rose or my gun." It all depends on whether she gets the system of one person, one vote.

I just finished a painting that foretells nuclear destruction. As far as the warming of the earth, the depletion of the ozone layer, the contamination of our water, earth, and air, you'd think, according to government spokespeople, that we have all the time in the world to act. Change will occur when people take action and not wait for others to do so. I am ready to appeal to my fellow artists. It has to start someplace.

After taking part in the demonstrations against the Vietnam War, I felt the next place to take my protest was my easel. We were involved in an illegitimate war, unlike, say, the Revolutionary War. There are many ways the story needs to be told, and I feel privileged to be a part of this exhibition, which presents at least forty different ways.

11. THE PLAYPEN, *1967, oil on board, 34 x 50 inches*

12. ISAIAH II:4, *1966, oil on canvas, 30 x 40 inches*

TRAN TRUNG TIN

On our first visit to the Art Association in Ho Chi Minh City, we encountered an extraordinary exhibition of the work of Tran Trung Tin. There were nine sculptures and forty-four small paintings, in oil on paper, each a jewel. His work is universal with a wide range of feelings from tragic to sad to ironic to funny. Trung Tin is a visual philosopher and poet, who one friend describes as "a bird in the desert." His titles are delightful, indicating an artist at home with words.

LT I have been told that you are self-taught.

TTT Yes, and I have been painting for twenty years. This is the first time my paintings have been shown to the public.

LT You have an extraordinary talent. Why did you start to paint?

Can you see in my paintings the love of peace?

TTT Through my paintings I can express my feelings. I wanted to commit suicide, but I controlled myself. I have made a painting about those feelings.

LT What did you do before you became an artist? Were you a soldier?

TTT Yes, during the war with the French. After that, I was a radio broadcaster and then an actor in Vietnamese cinema. Can you see in my paintings the love of peace?

LT It comes across very clearly. Let's talk about *All this Commotion*. It's one of my favorites. Why did you make this painting?

TTT Life, especially in Vietnam, has many commotions. The church is very quiet and makes a contrast.

LT Tell me about this painting of a group of ladies.

TTT It's called *An Unnamed Blue Note*. In life, there are a lot of women who are impassive. Maybe when they are in a bad state, they feel nothing.

LT Question in Broad Daylight is so beautiful in color, yet I see tension in this painting.

TTT Sometimes I sit quietly, and I hear a lot of questions from a lot of people.

LT The Last Time, with a lone figure and a cross, seems to be a painting of grief.

TTT It expresses the sadness of the lady who says goodbye to her boyfriend or husband, who died in the war.

LT Are you able to paint much?

TTT No, my health is bad. I became sick five years ago. I did prepare some paintings for this Art Association exhibition. I have a lot of paintings in my house.

LT I wish we could take all of the paintings with us. I know they would speak to American viewers.

46

13. THE LAST TIME, *1978,*
oil on photographic paper, 10 x 8 inches

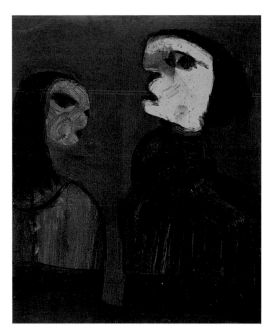

14. QUESTION IN BROAD DAYLIGHT, *1978*
oil on photographic paper, 11 x 8 1/2 inches

15. ALL THIS COMMOTION, *1980,*
oil on photographic paper, 7 7/8 x 9 7/8 inches

16. AN UNNAMED BLUE NOTE, *1979,*
oil on photographic paper, 8 x 10 inches

N G A N   C H A I

Ngan Chai is one of the younger artists in the exhibition. Although he joined the military before going to art school, he was talented enough to be an army artist. He made drawings and posters in his work with an army transportation unit. In 1982 the army sent him to study at the School of Fine Arts in Hanoi. He is the only artist in the show who is currently in the military, and he intends to stay "as long as the army requires me to stay." A standard career is twenty-five years but, he says, "I can stay longer if my health is good."

LT Your two works in the exhibition are quite different. We can get an idea of the range of your work. First the woodcut, what do you call it?

NC Transporting Guns to Long Dai. The artillery is being ferried across the river at night.

I wish the people who come to the exhibition will understand the war in Vietnam.

LT It is very effective. I like the idea that the second work is not about war at all. What is the title?

NC Cuban Cows at Moc Chau. It is a gouache painting.

LT Did these cows actually come from Cuba?

NC Yes, they are raising this breed here now and developing hybrids.

LT It is a charming and even an amusing painting because of the way you've captured, with facility, the nature of cows. The mountainous landscape is well painted. Have you seen art from other countries?

NC I have seen prints published in books of Russian landscape painting of the mountains and the sea. I have also seen two graphic art exhibitions from Czechoslovakia, one in 1984 and one in 1986.

LT What do you hope to say with your work?

NC I wish the people who come to the exhibition will understand the war in Vietnam.

17. Cuban Cows at Moc Chau, *1986,*
gouache on rice paper, 12 1/2 x 17 inches

18. Transporting Guns to Long Dai, *1984,*
woodcut on rice paper, 11 3/4 x 16 1/2 inches

NGUYEN THE MINH

At the time of our visit to Hanoi in Spring 1989, Nguyen The Minh was the president of the Fine Arts Department of the Ministry of Culture. He was given the position by the state, he says, because "as a painter I know this work." He also proved to be a capable administrator as he negotiated matters dealing with this exhibition.

LT Does your work take you to other countries?

NTM The Fine Arts Department is in charge of culture, literature, and art. I have arranged exhibitions to some socialist countries.

LT Do you have a chance to see the art in these countries?

We still have a lot of work to do for renovation, but the organization of the society is in very good order. At the same time, we lack materials. We expend much effort, but the results are still limited. People in our department and in our society try to improve everything for their lives and for their country.

NTM I may use a trip to visit a museum. When I was in the United States to discuss holding an exhibition there, I visited museums in San Francisco, Washington, Cleveland, Pittsburgh, and Los Angeles. In Moscow I visited a museum displaying modern art. Of the different kinds of art, the imaginative impresses me the most. I think much art from the Soviet Union and from France is very interesting. I particularly like Toulouse-Lautrec and Matisse.

LT What led you to become an artist?

NTM As a child I was always drawn to painting. My participation in the war against the French domination inspired my painting. When I worked in the Propaganda and Cultural Office in The Bak, I was recognized as talented enough to become a painter and was given permission to study at the School of Fine Arts in Hanoi.

LT I know you always paint on silk. What are your subjects?

NTM I am inspired by the mountain region of The Bak in the northwest of the Bien Phu area where I lived as a youth. The painting you have chosen, *Revisiting an Old Battle Site*, depicts Hill A1, where the last and most violent battle with the French was carried out. This painting does not show the battle. It recalls a visit I made in 1964, when I saw guerrillas training there for the American war.

LT What is the woman doing?

NTM She is pouring drinking water into a cup for the soldiers. We have a saying in Vietnam, "If you eat the fruit, you are one with the people who plant the tree." Whenever you drink the water, you become part of the source. If we are happy now, we have to think of those who made these opportunities.

19. REVISITING AN OLD BATTLE SITE, *1980, painting on silk, 32 1/2 x 55 inches*

NGUYEN NGHIA DUYEN

It is natural that Nguyen Nghia Duyen would become an artist proficient in wood-cut. His hometown is Dong Ho, a village famous for its woodcut artists. Now he teaches woodcut along with drawing at the School of Fine Arts in Hanoi. He took us on a tour of the facility, where students were hard at work learning the fundamentals.

Nghia Duyen's excellent drawing skills and his ability to capture the mood of a moment are apparent in his painting on silk entitled *Uncle Ho at the Border Campaign*.

NND He was the leader and chief of the army during the two wars. I made this impression of him after viewing many documents.

LT What did you do during the war?

ND Sometimes I fought with my comrades, but mostly I was an army writer and illustrator in the South. We had to print our newspapers under the ground in tunnels.

When I was a soldier, I always thought of the tradition of resistance against aggression, but now the war is over and people like me don't spend much time thinking of it.

LT The woodcut of Vietnamese soldiers entitled *Hanoi 1946* is very strong.

NND I made this one in 1984 on the occasion of the thirtieth anniversary of the liberation of Hanoi from the French.

LT Before we came to your country, many Vietnamese who live in America said we wouldn't find recent work about the war, that people wanted to forget about it and get on with their lives. Is this true?

NND When I was a soldier, I always thought of the tradition of resistance against aggression, but now the war is over and people like me don't spend much time thinking of it.

LT Now, what do you paint?

NND The peasants, the people in the countryside, and also the festivals of the temples and pagodas in the rural areas. The different villages hold their festivals at different times.

LT Do you have anything you'd like to add to our discussion?

NND I wish, in the future, that we could have more exhibitions so we can view as much as possible the art of the two countries.

20. HANOI 1946, *1984, woodcut on rice paper, 16 x 23 inches*

21. UNCLE HO AT THE BORDER CAMPAIGN 1950,
1984, painting on silk, 22 1/8 x 30 1/4 inches

PHAM NGUYEN HUNG

Pham Nguyen Hung is only now fulfilling a long-held dream of attending the School of Fine Arts in Hanoi. His job at the Social Welfare Ministry and his family responsibilities allow him to study only part time, three months a year for five years. The works in this exhibition were executed in 1971 during a three-month course in his army unit.

LT You actually had a drawing course in your army unit?

PNH Yes, all of the army branches have their own courses. They also teach creative writing , poetry, music, and popular performance. There are no classes at the frontier, just in the occupation area.

When I was a child many, many teachers told me I had talent, but I didn't have the opportunity to study in art school....I took my first art course in the army. All of the army branches have their own courses. They also teach creative writing, poetry, music, and popular performance.

LT You must have known before you took this course that you had artistic talent.

PNH When I was a child many, many teachers told me I had talent, but I didn't have the opportunity to study in art school. My parents died when I was a child. My oldest sister took care of me and my brothers and sisters.

LT The works in the show are beautifully drawn and seem especially accomplished considering you hadn't yet attended the School of Fine Arts. You are finally starting this year, at age forty-two. Is it customary for someone your age to go to art school?

PNH Many friends my age are in this school.

LT What subjects are you studying?

PNH Since it's my first year here, I have basic studies.

LT It looks like you already know how to do that work. Please tell me what you did in the army? How long were you in the army and were you in combat?

PNH I took part in anti-aircraft maneuvers in Hanoi in the North, Hai Phong in the South, and even in Laos. I was in the army for thirteen years, from 1962 to 1974.

LT That was almost the entire war. You told me that your wife died recently and that you have two children. Are you able to manage?

PNH In addition to working at the ministry, I have contracted to make drawings for book covers, calendars, and other such things.

LT At least it's related to art, and you're not driving a cyclo (bicycle cab) to make a living.

54

22. LOOKOUT POST FROM TREETOP (BASE CAMP), *1971,*
watercolor on rice paper, 15 7/8 x 8 inches

23. SOLDIERS COOKING AT THE BASE CAMP, *1971,*
watercolor on rice paper, 11 1/2 x 15 3/4 inches

★

C. DAVID THOMAS

David Thomas, organizer of this exhibition, is a man of enormous patience, commitment, and persistence. Undaunted by bureaucratic red tape, hours of letter writing, funding problems, and countless unexpected hitches, he never even considered quitting. He was driven by a desire to unite in peace the people of Vietnam and the United States and to change the official American policy against Vietnam.

In 1987, seventeen years after completing his tour of duty, Thomas returned to Vietnam with the United States–Indochina Reconciliation Project. He always knew he would go back. "I wanted to meet the people as a fellow citizen of the planet, to find out who these people were whom we supposedly hated."

The one image of the war that has never left me is that of the children. They were the true victims of that war. When I returned to Vietnam in 1987, it was again the children whose faces would not leave me. They are the continuing tragedy of the war. Adults make war and children inherit the aftermath.

His first encounter with Vietnam came in June 1968, when the young draftee was sent over to make blueprints of roads, bunkers, and military buildings. Six months later, Thomas became a jeep driver. He never had what he calls a "combat role," but, he notes, "You couldn't avoid being in combat, at some point. It was that kind of war. I always carried my M-16. I felt vulnerable. When I was driving the jeep in the mountains, we were often shelled and ambushed. I didn't fire the rifle much, but it was my security blanket. I wasn't shooting at any particular target but just trying to make a lot of noise to scare off the enemy. I was fortunate that I never had face-to-face contact with the enemy, where it would be him or me."

Thomas did have personal contact with South Vietnamese. It was his job to take his unit's soiled linens and clothes to a family-run laundry. He became quite close to the family and enjoyed clowning around with the three little daughters. Today he still thinks about going back to Pleiku to try to find them.

For Thomas, "the greatest tragedy of the war is the legacy left behind for the children of Vietnam." He has done many drawings of Vietnamese children, such as the poignant one in the exhibition of a boy with barbed wire wrapped around his head. Thomas could not envision a show on Vietnam without its dominant icon, Ho Chi Minh. *Uncle Ho* is his portrait of the man he first feared and hated, then recognized as "great." The "tragedy of the American war in Vietnam could have been avoided," Thomas says, "if our leaders in the early sixties had only taken time to understand Ho's motivation."

The exhibition, the result of hard work by many people, realizes part of Thomas's dream to do "something of significance, beyond the normal day-to-day things, that leaves a lasting change in the world for the better."

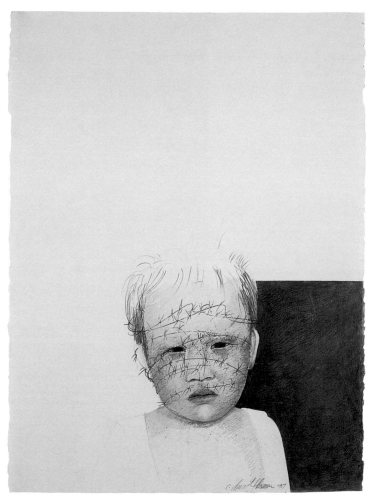

24. STANDING FIGURE, *1989,*
mixed media on rag paper, 30 x 22 inches

25. BAC HO, *1990,*
mixed media on rag paper, 29 1/2 x 41 3/4 inches

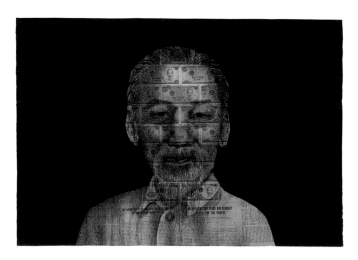

TIN LY

Tin Ly is the only American exhibitor who was born in Vietnam. He is of Chinese extraction but, like other Chinese living in Vietnam, he and his family were forced during the Diem regime to take Vietnamese citizenship or lose their fortunes and be expelled.

During the Tet Offensive, Ly, his parents, and his sisters hid in an underground cellar. "At night we heard people shouting, tanks rolling around, and even bullets on the roof. It's hard to forget those noises. It went on for several days. We saw a lot of dead bodies. I was only fourteen years old."

In 1971, at age eighteen, Tin Ly was able to come alone to the United States to study at Indiana University. He majored in voice but audited art classes and sought critiques from the studio faculty. Although he did graduate work in scene design, he rejected that profession for full-time painting.

I learned a lot about myself when painting these pieces, especially about my ability after all this time to portray violence. My intent was not to describe but to let these memories emerge in the paint itself.

Tin Ly's series of ten paintings on the Vietnam War started in 1980. One powerful work was inspired by the famous Eddie Adams photograph of a Viet Cong soldier holding a gun to a prisoner's head. Tin Ly explains, "It's a key visual communication throughout the world. I didn't really paint the form. There are no features. I allowed the paint to do the job. It just naturally ran and dripped. I call it *Gunshot Heard around the World*." In another work, the dark and somber *Moonlit Night,* two figures embrace each other in a gesture of comfort. "I can imagine the loneliness of soldiers on the battlefield. Some may be wounded physically or emotionally. They need someone with them, but often they are alone. In both paintings, I refer to all wars and all soldiers all over the world."

Being in this exhibition is especially significant for Tin Ly. "I feel that a load of guilt is off my shoulders. The guilt was from my coming to this country when my thoughts were tied to my family in Vietnam. The kind of loneliness I had is projected in *Moonlit Night*. For this painting to be shown in Vietnam is fine. I don't feel politically blacklisted. The motive for the show, I assume, is the expression of the human side, the suffering, and then the healing." He adds, "The experience of this war should transcend all our differences, be they political, philosophical, religious, or racial. And the art that we produce should reflect this attitude."

In 1978 most of Tin Ly's family moved to Australia, where his parents soon died. Though he has little family in Vietnam, Tin Ly would like to return "one of these days" because, in his words, "I just want to see the country again."

26. GUNSHOT HEARD AROUND THE WORLD, *1985, acrylic on canvas, 51 x 70 1/4 inches*

27. MOONLIT NIGHT, *1985,*
acrylic on canvas, 62 x 55 1/2 inches

James R. Cannata

For James R. Cannata, the exhaustive media coverage of the Vietnam War made the images blur and the war seem an ordinary news event. Not until years later, when he rediscovered the images in books, did he get the full impact of the horror of the war.

JRC It was as if I were seeing those images for the first time. The reality hit me. I wanted to capture all the emotions that became real for me, maybe to cause other people to see these things fresh. We had and still have a very erroneous idea of what war is, romanticized with notions of heroism.

LT You must have been young when you entered the army.

I wanted to capture all the emotions that became real for me, maybe to cause other people to see these things fresh. We had and still have a very erroneous idea of what war is, romanticized with notions of heroism.

JRC I got my draft notice on my twentieth birthday. I was really scared, as were my friends. We thought we would be sent to Vietnam. Actually, I ended up in Germany. I had mixed emotions about the involvement in Vietnam. Many people I knew and respected felt we should be there, and many others thought we shouldn't. I was brought up to respect adults and my teachers, and when I saw my classmates challenging them, it was a strange experience for me. I didn't know what side to be on.

LT But you did make a decision.

JRC Yes, but it took a long while. I did intend these works to be a judgment and to make others aware of the brutality of war.

LT Your photographs are moving and frightening, but they are also very painterly.

JRC I started out as a painter, but when I got to college I became more and more involved in photography. But I missed the direct interaction I was able to get with painting. So I make a painting on any transparent or translucent surface like glass, acetate, paper, or fabric. Besides paint, I use such things as printed paper, Magic Markers, anything that is translucent and has color and texture. Then I project light through the negative to expose the photographic paper.

LT Let's talk about the imagery in these two pieces, which derive from a famous photograph by Eddie Adams. In a spare, gestural way you convey the essence of a universal tragedy.

JRC They are from a series called *They Killed Many of My Men*, which is what the South Vietnam general offered as an explanation for the execution of a Viet Cong soldier. One image depicts the execution; in the other image, the South Vietnamese soldiers lead the captured Viet Cong to the general.

LT The prisoner is so skeletal. It's quite terrifying.

JRC And they're taunting him. What really struck me was that someone could just come up and take someone else's life. It just floored me that one person has the power to decide that another person's life is over.

28. THEY KILLED MANY OF MY MEN #1, *1983, color photograph/cliché verre, 17 x 21 inches*

29. THEY KILLED MANY OF MY MEN #3, *1983, color photograph/cliché verre, 17 x 21 inches*

DAVID SCHIRM

Tim O'Brien, in his book *The Things They Carried*, described wartime Vietnam as "a place where men died because of carelessness and gross stupidity." In David Schirm's experience, the war was indeed a tragic comedy of errors. He enlisted because he hoped to direct his participation away from combat into something positive by going to Officers Candidate School in engineering. The strategy backfired when he was dismissed from OCS for letting his platoon eat ice cream bars.

Even before he was sent to Vietnam, he understood that the American involvement was "corrupt beyond hope." When he arrived, he was in no mood to cooperate. His experiences sound like episodes of *M*A*S*H*.

"An engineering brigade grabbed me off the plane. I was their clerk for only a week because I refused to learn the filing system. Then I was a jeep driver for a major, but I either went too fast or too slow. The final blow came during a typhoon. To be 'cool' he tied his prized jungle hat over his head instead of under his chin. It blew off into a minefield. When I refused to retrieve it, my jeep job ended." After helping to supervise the construction of temporary buildings that "were left to rot, unused," Schirm was transferred to a cartography outfit, where he continued to frustrate the authorities. "They wouldn't allow me to go out of the trailer to view the China Sea. So, I'd open my door and look out. They padlocked the door. I had to stay in my own trailer and do only government business. When there was none, I had to sit and do nothing."

There's a lot of emotion connected to this show, with the participation of the Vietnamese. It's a healing show. It makes up for when you got home and didn't get the parade.

One of Schirm's "contributions to the war" was making going-away presents for officers. "I talked them into accepting drawings rather than plaques. Captains and below got drawings in black and white. Majors and above got color. It was absurd."

Schirm also became fatalistic about the danger. "I understood there was major irony at work here. Our side was not on our side. They were so inept. One night, when there was some movement in the swamp, I called in for flares. Forty-five minutes later they got one up, and of course nothing was out there. We were sitting ducks."

Schirm's works in the exhibition are about the irony of war. "*Critic's Choice, Critic's Choice* shows somebody being saved who could just as easily have died. In *A Poem for All Wars*, a soldier's desperate appeal for his life depends on the knee-jerk reaction of the captors." Schirm believes that making art about the war is "a kind of healing, whether it is venting rage, expressing sorrow, or having a dark-hearted laugh." His drawings all have a cartoon quality because that "helps to diffuse emotions so that nobody gets hurt for real this time."

30. CRITIC'S CHOICE, CRITIC'S CHOICE,
1983, mixed media on paper, 30 x 22 inches

31. A POEM FOR ALL WARS, *1983*
mixed media on paper, 22 x 30 inches

MAY STEVENS

With her *Big Daddy* series May Stevens created a symbol for the bullheaded, unreasoning male who bought, without question, the government line on the war in Vietnam. Many of her feminist friends, however, saw in Big Daddy a broader statement. With his elongated, bullet-shaped head, he is an icon of male power, a phallic image.

MS When I heard this reaction, I said, "Oh, that's interesting." It was not my conscious decision. I considered the paintings to be anti-establishment. But I accepted their interpretation of phallic power.

LT Why did you decide to take up the subject of the Vietnam War in your work?

MS I was involved in the civil rights and antiwar movements. It was really very consuming. There were lots of meetings and we went to Washington every spring to demonstrate. I heard Martin Luther King's "I have a dream" speech. I participated in the Los Angeles Peace Tower and in Angry Arts Week. My social life, my political life, and my studio life were the same.

LT Tell me how the *Big Daddy* series began.

MS It started with a portrait of my father, who was pro-war and pro-establishment. He was also racist and anti-Semitic, without ever doing anything about it. He was not outspoken. He was a regular, reticent New England guy. I started with a portrait of my father in which I showed him as a middle American in his undershirt, with his arms folded against his chest, and a blank television screen behind him. I called it *Prime Time*. It expressed my disappointment and anger with my father and those like him. They were the people supporting the war.

The great thing about working on the *Big Daddy* series was taking the figure through its paces. In the early work I showed him naked, as a diplomat with a derby and gray suede gloves and an attaché case. Soon I thought of him as a paper doll and dressed him in different clothes. I combined the art influences around me—pop, hard edge, color field, cartoons. I would say these paintings have no composition. Things are lined up flush with the canvas. I would say they have no color because they are red, white, and blue. They are not modulated or subtle. I had a great time designing them and using pure, flat color. As time went on, I began to long for subtlety.

LT Your work has a lot of variety. It's muralistic and it's intimate. It ranges from protest paintings to this luscious landscape of a canal.

MS Politics is part of my life but not the whole story. I'm interested in subtlety, in people, in human relationships, in feeling, in poetry. That's a big statement!

The series started with a portrait of my father, who was pro-war and pro-establishment, ...in which I showed him as a middle American in his undershirt, with his arms folded against his chest, and a blank television screen behind him. It expressed my disappointment and anger with my father and those like him. They were the people supporting the war.

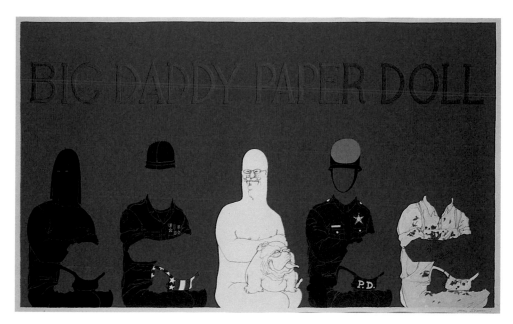

32. Big Daddy Paper Doll, *1971, gouache on paper, 21 x 35 inches*

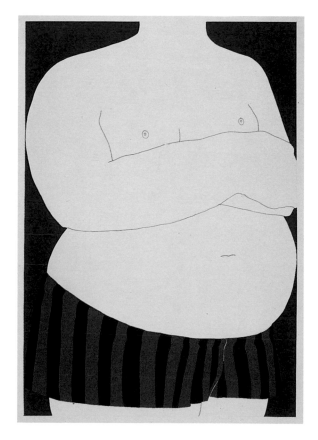

33. Big Daddy in Shorts, *1970,
gouache on paper, 30 x 22 1/2 inches*

DAVID SMITH

Chance was horribly and palpably real in Vietnam. My paintings contain violence, not that of napalm or white phosphorus or claymore mines, but the violence of helplessness in the face of chance. They are altarpieces and icons because, although objects of contemplation, they historically contain the violence of crucifixion or martyrdom. The violence does not repel, so the viewer can contemplate and recognize my acts of memory. The viewer will know that I am his memory of the war, and that he must not forget me.

Soon after graduating from high school, David Smith joined the Marines and shipped out to Vietnam. The war was for him a "first trauma" that he repeats "over and over again" in his work. Through his paintings he is trying to claim and reorder some of the chaos of that time.

DS My work is a way of controlling violence and trying to grasp some meaning out of a random, chaotic event. I use images from the war whose occurrence and placement in a field are determined randomly by computer. The randomness is a metaphor for war. What happens in war has little to do with your skill and courage. It has to do with chance. So how can it mean anything? In Vietnam, if someone got blown away, we went out on ambush again at night. It didn't mean a damn thing.

LT You were quite young when you joined the Marines. Did you believe in the war?

DS No, not even from the beginning. A lot of my friends in the Marines felt the same way, that it was not a thing we should be doing. Part of what informs my work today is the conflict of experiencing the closest feelings and the best relationships and connectedness to the people I was fighting next to and, at the next moment, experiencing the greatest horror, degradation, and self-hate because of the destruction. Going to that war has made it very difficult for many of us to grow up.

LT What is amazing to me is that, in view of your obvious and continuing anguish about your war experience, your work is very beautifully painted and seductive. The military ribbons glorify war.

DS That is my conflict. And yet, violence is very hard to paint. You look at brutal war pictures in newspapers and you turn away. An icon of the crucifixion with all its gold and fine execution has both a horror and a beauty that keep you there in contemplation. I know I run the risk of glorification. What you see in my paintings is gold with numbers on it. The war was fought over money with numbers of bodies.

You know, I am *sick* of the Vietnam War. It's always on my mind. I'd like to think of something else.

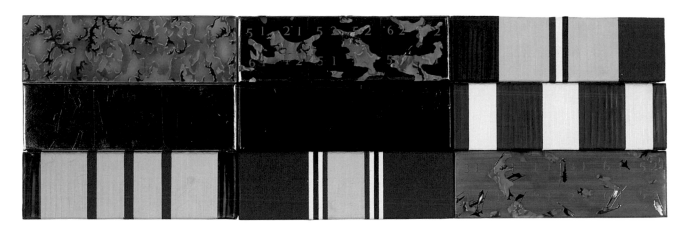

34. Untitled, *1990, egg tempura, gold and aluminum leaf, encaustic, and bole on Norcore, 8 1/4 x 26 inches*

★

VU GIANG HUONG

Vu Giang Huong is a strong presence in the art world of Vietnam. Since 1962 she has been in charge of silk and woodcut at the School of Fine Arts in Hanoi, where she had received her art education, and from 1977 to 1987 was vice-director of the school. She was recently elected vice-director of the Fine Arts Association, which has 779 members throughout the nation and organizes exhibitions in both Vietnam and other countries.

VGH I was a teacher in this college during the war. My students and I volunteered to be with army units. On each trip I took around ten students for two to five months. First, we drew the activities of the soldiers; second, we helped the army artist make posters; third, we exhibited our works to help morale; and, finally, we helped rebuild bombed-out roads on the Ho Chi Minh Trail. We slept in stone caves. Over their objections, women students went to safer places.

LT I assume that the woodcuts *Ham Rong Bridge* and *Ferry Landing at Night* are from personal experiences with the army units.

VGH They are from drawings I did on the site.

LT It seems to me there are very few professional women artists in Vietnam.

VGH That's true. We have some one hundred women artists working in graphic arts in all of Vietnam. It is not easy to become a member of the Fine Arts Association. It's hard for women to pass the examination to get into the college. About twenty percent of the students are women. After graduating they have to create art that will qualify them for membership in the association. I think that Vietnamese women are very skilled and have good ideas on art. But during the war they not only participated, but also had to take care of children. Even now women have a lot to do. They work in offices and have all the family work. They don't have the opportunity to do good art.

I think that Vietnamese women are very skilled and have good ideas on art. But during the war they not only participated, but also had to take care of children. Even now women have a lot to do. They work in offices and have all the family work. They don't have the opportunity to do good art.

68

35. Ferry Landing at Night, *1965, woodcut on rice paper, 10 1/2 x 16 inches*

36. Ham Rong Bridge, *1970, woodcut on rice paper, 12 x 16 7/8 inches*

★

NGUYEN THE HUU

Nguyen The Huu's homeland is in Dien Tien Province, near the old imperial city of Hue. After attending the School of Fine Arts in Hanoi, he went into the army in 1970. As an artillery soldier he took part in the Ho Chi Minh Campaign. Sometimes he managed to find time to paint. He recorded the everyday activities of the war without the explicit violence. "I think it's a good idea to have an exhibition in the United States about the war that doesn't make people think of cruelty. There are so many war paintings showing people killing each other with swords, guns, and bombs." The Huu made many paintings that were lost when his friends, who were transporting them to safety in Hanoi, came under attack.

Of the paintings of that era, one is especially gripping. The artist gives this explanation of *Tropical Trees*. "In 1975, during the Ho Chi Minh Campaign, I went through a barbed wire fence and saw this strange object. At first I didn't know what it was. Later, I learned it was some American communications equipment, an antenna. We called it a tropical tree. Actually, it had hand grenades hanging from it. It was a trap."

I think it's a good idea to have an exhibition in the United States about the war that doesn't make people think of cruelty. There are so many war paintings showing people killing each other with swords, guns, and bombs.

As lethal as this object is, the drawing of it has a whimsical quality. Perhaps it is the use of colored pens for an image with dangling beer cans that makes the device seem a playful mobile sculpture. This lightness, especially when set against the abandoned boot and helmet of an American soldier, accentuates the grimness of the trap. The Huu made this colored drawing on site in Da Nang.

His second piece in the exhibition, *Passing the Checkpoint*, is a skillfully executed gouache on paper. It depicts the ferry area on the Xang River in his hometown. The low point of view gives an imposing aspect to the military trucks rumbling along the road.

Today The Huu works as a painter in the Cultural Department of the army. He is at liberty to paint whatever he likes, "even my family, landscapes, and the people." He also works from documentation he made when in combat. During the war he had the opportunity to show such work, but not afterward. "In Vietnam they hold exhibitions on many subjects and sometimes on a particular subject, but not on the activities of the war." Although in school The Huu was instructed in many styles from different European countries and was free to choose any style he wished, he believes "the best way to paint is to use natural color and the traditional style of Vietnam."

37. TROPICAL TREES, *1975, ballpoint pen on rice paper, 7 1/4 x 7 3/4 inches*

38. PASSING THE CHECKPOINT, *1972,*
gouache on rice paper, 15 x 21 1/4 inches

★

T R I N H   K I M   V I N H

Trinh Kim Vinh lives her life as an artist with enthusiasm and determination. These attitudes are necessary to maintain a career in art in any country but especially in Vietnam during the war and while raising three children. Kim Vinh credits her late husband, the former Minister of Cultural Information, with being very supportive and for insisting that she go to the site of her subject, regardless of the distance. Today Kim Vinh teaches painting at the School of Fine Arts in Ho Chi Minh City and continues to create lithographs.

LT For many reasons, women artists tend to have a harder time than men in the United States. Is this true also in Vietnam?

TKV In my country, there are a lot of difficulties for women artists. But, since I love art, I must overcome the obstacles.

LT You have three grown children. It must have been difficult, when they were little, to make your art.

TKV Yes, especially because I had to raise them alone, when my husband was in the battlefield. But I raised them and painted, too. When I went somewhere to paint, my children went with me.

Many Vietnamese artists want to form an organization that bids farewell to weapons. Just this morning many art teachers met to plan an exhibition using pieces of weaponry to create pictures symbolic of peace.

LT Please tell me about your education.

TKV After I graduated from the College of Fine Arts in Hanoi, where I studied painting, I went to East Germany for three years to learn lithography. I received a degree and graduated with honors.

LT Where did you create the two lithographs chosen for exhibition?

TKV I printed both of them myself at Dresden University. One is called *Female Soldier Stands Guard near the Sea*. I saw her at sunset as I sat by the sea. The light from the setting sun fell upon her. It made a great impression on me. When I went home, I painted it. The other lithograph I call *Operation through the Jungles*. I drew it in 1968 and printed it later in East Germany.

Please permit me to comment on your efforts with this exhibition. I believe it will show many people in the United States more about the war in Vietnam and about the Vietnamese people. The two countries will get closer. It's good propaganda for both countries. It is most important for American and Vietnamese artists to get to know each other and to do good things through art. Many Vietnamese artists want to form an organization that bids farewell to weapons. Just this morning many art teachers met to plan an exhibition using pieces of weaponry to create pictures symbolic of peace.

39. OPERATION THROUGH THE JUNGLES, *1973, lithograph on rag paper, 13 x 17 inches*

40. FEMALE SOLDIER STANDS GUARD NEAR THE SEA, *1973,*
lithograph on rag paper, 13 1/8 x 12 7/8 inches

★

T R A N   T E

Tran Te was born in Tang Hua Province in 1936 and now lives in Hanoi. While in the army, he went to the School of Fine Arts in Hanoi. An earnest and gentle man, Tran Te is gratified that he could, through his work as an army artist in both the French and American wars, raise the morale of his fellow soldiers.

TT I was not in the fighting. I worked as one of the people who organized exhibitions. These exhibitions were to encourage the soldiers. I also made documentary paintings. The situations around me, during the wars, inspired me to paint.

LT As an army artist, were you expected to paint specific things, or were you left to make your own decisions?

Here in my country people made every effort to do their part in the war. Now, the situation has changed. Our country is at peace, so that even the army tries to do everything to keep peace.

TT I did work of my own choosing.

LT On the Way to an Operation shows a woman looking into a microscope, and there are soldiers marching by. Tell me about this subject.

TT We were traveling on the Ho Chi Minh Trail in Thum Sum in the Long Range Mountains. I made this painting in an army medical station.

LT Why did you choose this semi-abstract manner of painting?

TT I could simplify the subject in order to emphasize the movement of the soldiers through the forest to the frontier and into a dangerous situation. It seemed right to paint a medical station that cares for the health of these soldiers.

LT In *Spring at the Border* the composition directs the movement up and into space.

TT That's right. The piece was painted for the Lunar New Year festival. The soldiers, who are returning from battle, are in bad condition. At the same time, they celebrate the Tet festival by putting flowers in a shell casing.

LT That is a very moving idea. How long does it take you to do a painting like this one on silk?

TT I spend a lot of time thinking about what subject to paint. It takes much longer than the time spent painting, which is a few weeks to a month.

74

41. SPRING AT THE BORDER, *1973,*
painting on silk, 28 x 21 1/2 inches

42. ON THE WAY TO AN OPERATION, *1973,*
painting on silk, 29 x 22 1/2 inches

ARNOLD TRACHTMAN

Arnold Trachtman grew up during the thirties and forties in Lynn, Massachusetts, a shoe-manufacturing town with strong union affiliations and a history of radical politics. At a young age he became sensitive to injustice, both as a witness to the struggles of the working class around him and as the target of the religious intolerance of schoolmates.

From the beginning Trachtman's paintings responded to the gross misuses of authority in government. He expresses this theme not only with satirical, blunt subject matter, but also through strident color and aggressive, disorienting compositions.

There is a consistent conspiracy to erase history. Artists should prevent that from happening in whatever way they can. All artists don't need to do political work, but they should be conscious of what's going on. Politics, whether we like it or not, determines art.

LT What drives you to use your art for protest?

AT For me, painting has been the means to communicate and explore why some people make other people do things they shouldn't do. I'm not interested in bemoaning man's inhumanity to man. That's too easy. I want to know who and why—who's really guilty and who has profited from it. A modern artist is a questioner and a criticizer. We're no longer painting for the church and for kings, so why shouldn't we take a critical view?

LT When did you become aware of these issues?

AT In high school, I became aware that the myths we were raised on are contradictions of the real world. We were learning about the Bill of Rights, yet our own Capitol was surrounded by an enormous ghetto.

LT During the sixties you took part in protests on behalf of civil rights and against the American involvement in Vietnam. When did these subjects get into your work?

AT My show in 1964 dealt directly with Vietnam. It included one of these paintings: the one of a lone soldier with cartridge bandoleers hanging down his back as he walks into a green hell. I was opposed to the war but not to the poor souls who had to go over there.

LT You have always crusaded. Don't you ever get discouraged?

AT There is a consistent conspiracy to erase history. Artists should prevent that from happening in whatever way they can. All artists don't need to do political work, but they should be conscious of what's going on. Politics, whether we like it or not, determines art. Everything in the world is politicized; nothing is pure. A lot of people don't want to think about that. It's ugly, but I'd rather choose my politics than act out someone else's.

43. Untitled, *1972*,
oil on canvas, 60 1/4 x 50 1/8 inches

44. The Defender, *1965*,
oil on canvas, 50 x 36 1/4 inches

BUI TAN HUNG

It was not a simple matter to select only two woodcuts from Bui Tan Hung's portfolio. He is skilled in the medium and is a facile draftsman. His depictions of battles are filled with a sense of urgency and dire threat.

After serving in the army during the war with the French, he went to Hanoi where, in 1955, he embarked on eight years of art education at the School of Fine Arts.

LT What did you do during the war with the Americans?

BTH I was an army artist with the North Vietnamese. During the war I went everywhere in Vietnam and Laos to paint. In Tay Village in 1968 there was a terrible fight between the Americans and the soldiers from the North. In my woodcut I wanted to describe the battle and the courage of the Northern fighters.

LT It's a very stirring picture. The red definitely contributes an emotional effect, and the marks you make seem to describe the sounds of battle. In the other picture, *Attacking Tan Son Nhat Airport*, you really convey action by repeating the diagonals of the running men in the rising smoke from the burning American aircraft. What did you do after the war?

BTH I came back to the South, where I worked as a censor for the import and export of art. Now I work at the Museum of Fine Arts in Ho Chi Minh City.

LT Do you still make woodcuts?

In my woodcut I wanted to describe the battle and the courage of the Northern fighters.

BTH Yes, but sometimes I work in lacquer.

LT What are your subjects now?

BTH Beautiful scenery, a pagoda, the culture, and the people. I've made a lot of woodcuts about the war, and I hope that many people in other countries will know about these works.

78

45. Attacking Tan Son Nhat Airport, *1968, woodcut on rice paper, 9 1/2 x 12 3/4 inches*

46. The Battle at Tay Village, *1968,*
woodcut on rice paper, 11 x 15 inches

QUACH VAN PHONG

The Fine Arts Association in Vietnam, in contrast to the private, nonprofit groups with similar names in the United States, is an official government agency. Since 1985 Quach Van Phong has been the secretary general of the Fine Arts Association in Ho Chi Minh City. He oversees with energy and efficiency the association's three successful factories. They produce artists' materials, porcelain, and lacquerware. As one might expect, Quach Phong has little time to paint.

After studying at the School of Fine Arts in Hanoi from 1955 to 1963, he served in the army. In 1966, as a civilian connected with the military, he became a writer and illustrator for the army newspaper. In 1973 he was wounded and sent to Hanoi. He returned to Saigon in 1975, where he started working at the Art Association.

Quach Phong has the only lacquer painting in the exhibition, *The Stone Den at Ba Ra Mountain*. Compared to many other lacquer paintings in the Fine Arts Museum in Ho Chi Minh City, his is a fine example of a traditional medium employed with individuality. It appears to be a painstaking technique, especially since his work contains mosaics of cracked eggshells. He explains, "I started it in 1975 and finished it in 1985. I painted it from a sketch I made in the war. It shows a stone den in Ba Ra Mountain. At the time the soldiers lived in the den. The conditions were terrible."

Quach Phong is "very happy" to be a part of the exhibition. Yet, he feels, "it is very strange to me that you bring this work to your country, that you have the courage to let everyone know about the reality of the war in Vietnam."

It is very strange to me that you bring this work to your country, that you have the courage to let everyone know about the reality of the war in Vietnam. I hope the next exhibition will be about peace.

80

47. ON THE WAY TO AN OPERATION, *1972, gouache on rice paper, 16 1/2 x 24 inches*

48. THE STONE DEN AT BA RA MOUNTAIN, *1980, lacquer on wood, 24 x 32 inches*

NGUYEN MINH DINH

It is unfortunate that the logistics of this exhibition precluded sculpture, because that is Nguyen Minh Dinh's primary medium. He attended the School of Industrial Arts in Hanoi from 1950 to 1954, where he learned how to make lacquer in different ways. From 1958 to 1963 he was employed in film workshops. He joined the army in 1963 and was assigned duty as a typist.

NMD As an army typist, I didn't do fine art, but I got information from the battlefield. I knew the reported casualties. So many people were killed. I did my typing in a stone cave, separated from the battles.

In 1966 I applied to join the operations of the army and soon had good opportunities to make drawings. At other times I carried supplies to the army at the front. I was stopped many times by American attacks. I lived and worked with my friends, the soldiers. Those times inspired my drawings. After the liberation, I made from memory some cement sculptures of those soldiers who died in the war. They are now in the Long Range Mountains.

LT Do you now have enough time for your art?

NMD To support my own work I must spend time doing sculptures from models for export to foreign countries.

LT It sounds similar to the plight of many American artists. Let's talk about the very effective drawing of the ferry in the moonlight.

NMD At night I stayed in a cave with a lamp and made a sketch of what I saw. I developed it soon after. It is a supply ferry on the Bac River.

LT Is the defoliation of the trees from bombs or Agent Orange?

NMD From the bombs. In other places everything was destroyed, there are no trees at all.

LT The other picture shows a very common event, a soldier getting a haircut. It takes on a poignancy in an army camp.

NMD I am eager to make hundreds of sculptures showing the activities of the soldiers on The Trail. I think it would be very good if I had the opportunity of an invitation from the United States to do sculptures describing the activities of the soldiers during the war.

LT I do hope you get a chance to make such sculptures and, perhaps, in collaboration with an American.

NMD You should prepare a good place to show them, similar to the forest in Vietnam. When I was a soldier, I got no salary. I would be willing to make a hundred sculptures for no payment at all.

My main medium is sculpture, mostly in cement, although I can carve stone and wood. We meet with difficulties in making sculpture in Vietnam because we don't have enough materials.

82

49. THE HAIRCUT, *1967, black ink on paper, 13 3/4 x 15 3/4 inches*

50. BAC FERRY LANDING, *1967,*
black ink on paper, 17 1/4 x 23 1/2 inches

★

BENNY ANDREWS

Benny Andrews grew up in a part of Georgia where, for poor whites and blacks, the only ticket to a good education and the only escape from a life of menial labor was the military. "The GI Bill provided the only opportunity to move out of our situation. Also, I was raised in an environment where you automatically served your country. In a poor area, the media—newspaper, radio, and later television—have a great influence. They portrayed the military as glamorous."

After serving in the Korean War, Andrews went to the school of the Art Institute of Chicago. While there he read Norman Mailer's *The Naked and the Dead* and Erich Remarque's *All Quiet on the Western Front*. According to Andrews, "These two books formed my thinking about war, that it's an immoral and irrational thing. Wars are not started, as people claim, for patriotic reasons, but for economic reasons. People are manipulated and used for these purposes. A lot of my disappointment about people who were against the war in Vietnam was that they were only against that war and not against all wars per se."

I never set out intentionally to do the Vietnam War. It just bled into my work while I was doing other subjects relating to my life....My Vietnam paintings were about war in general....Until we see war as a continuous, universal threat, we will be picking our wars and forgetting about them afterward.

LT When did you first do work relating to the war in Vietnam?

BA It was when I was involved in the civil rights and anti-Vietnam War protests. They overlapped. It was a natural subject for me. What is active for me now is my protest work about South Africa. The Vietnam War is over for me. I never set out to do the Vietnam War. It just bled into my work while I was doing other subjects relating to my life. My art is an expression of myself. It's a very selfish thing, but I hope that whatever I do will speak to other people. My Vietnam paintings were about war in general. Since the Civil War, we've always fought our wars someplace else. As the song says, "Over There." Until we see war as a continuous, universal threat, we will be picking our wars and forgetting about them afterward.

LT Do you have any thoughts about this show?

BA Now we can show this work about Vietnam because it's no threat to society. The time to have taken the stand was when the problem existed. Some people feel that art should not deal with protest or social issues, that it makes art debased. The act of doing this show is important; the interaction between people is important. Hopefully, it will be a link in a chain of many cultural connections. You can never underestimate the impact of the arts. Often, art is the first and only thing that can make an inroad into coming to grips with a tragedy like Vietnam.

84

51. War Baby, *1968,*
oil and collage on canvas,
35 1/2 x 25 1/2 inches

52. War Mementos, *1966,*
oil on canvas, 19 1/2 x 23 1/2 inches

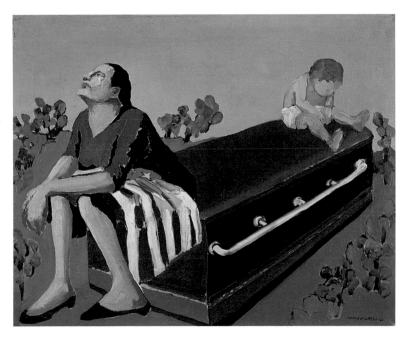

★

TRAN THANH LAM

One gets the sense that Tran Thanh Lam feels isolated from the international art world. He would like to know what's going on out there, and he would like to be a part of it. He has, however, taken a good look at twentieth-century Western European art.

LT Your work suggests to me that you are familiar with Fernand Léger.

TTL Yes, I like Léger, Matisse, Miró, Klee, Picasso, and I admire the art of Mexico—Rivera, Siqueiros, Orozco.

LT Soldier Playing a Guitar has some of the stylization of Léger, and *Bonfire* has an interesting surface that reminds me of the work of one of the American artists in the show.

TTL I would like to have a relationship with the art of Americans. We are very eager to study the sentiments of your culture. We lack information about American painting, so we can't study the techniques.

I like Léger, Matisse, Miró, Klee, Picasso, and I admire the art of Mexico—Rivera, Siqueiros, Orozco....I would like to have a relationship with the art of Americans....I want my paintings to be modern and international.

LT Tell me something about your background. When did you start painting?

TTL I started as a child, and I received an award in Germany for a painting in an exhibition for children. I studied at the Fine Arts schools in Hanoi and Ho Chi Minh City. From 1970 to 1975 I worked in Quan Tri Province as an illustrator for the North Vietnamese army newspaper.

LT Do you now have much time for your art?

TTL I paint every afternoon, but in the morning I must work in the factory of the Fine Arts Association that produces brushes and pigments.

I want my paintings to be modern and international. I'd like to have my own exhibition in your country and also one with my close friends. I'm very glad to get my paintings overseas to the United States and to have the opportunity to get acquainted with other artists and other paintings.

86

53. SOLDIER PLAYING A GUITAR, *1976, gouache on paper, 29 1/2 x 41 inches*

54. BONFIRE, *1976, oil on canvas, 31 x 44 1/2 inches*

Nguyen Tuan Khanh (Rung)

Nguyen Tuan Khanh is an outgoing and generous man who insisted on giving each of us a painting of our own choosing. The gift to me is a gestural and experimental painting of a head in which the forms are scratched through the paint to the supporting paper. It is an imaginative and poetic interpretation and is signed, as is all of Tuan Khanh's work, with the name Rung, a nickname meaning "poet."

LT You have such an ease with oil paint. When did you start painting?

NTK When I was about seven or eight years old. From 1960 to 1964 I went to the School of Fine Arts in Hue.

LT Were you also in the army as a military artist?

NTK Yes, for five years from 1970 to 1975. I was a soldier of the former regime in the South. After the revolution, from 1975 to 1980, I was put in a reeducation camp. When I was released, I took up painting again.

LT Do you have another job as well?

NTK I just paint. It is my job. Sometimes I sell my paintings and sometimes I can't.

LT Are you able to support your three children with your paintings?

NTK No, I can't. My wife is a worker.

I paint over posters or pictures from magazines. The subject doesn't matter because I use them only as a ground on which to paint. Sometimes some of the original colors show through.

LT I like the freedom in your paintings. The direction seems to be different from the other work we've seen. Your work has some feeling of French painting—Picasso, Chagall—especially in *Candle of Peace*. Have you been inspired by any other artists?

NTK If I am influenced, it is not consciously.

LT It appears these works are painted over photographs or posters. Am I right?

NTK Yes, I paint over posters or pictures from magazines. The subject doesn't matter because I use them only as a ground on which to paint. Sometimes some of the original colors show through.

LT Do you have much chance to exhibit your work here or in other countries?

NTK Yes, I have opportunities to exhibit here in the Art Association. And my work was shown in Washington, DC, in 1965. I wish to say that it is an honor to be selected for this exhibition.

55. CANDLE OF PEACE, *1988, oil on magazine photograph, 10 x 13 1/8*

56. UNTITLED, *1989,*
oil on magazine photograph,
10 3/4 x 8 inches

RICHARD J. OLSEN

As a teenager Richard J. Olsen was admittedly a "jock." He threw himself into competitive wrestling and weightlifting and majored in physical education in college. In the ROTC program he achieved a commission and a civil pilot's license. He fulfilled his three-year obligation to the army by attending flight school.

There was, however, another side to his education. When he found he needed a few credits to graduate, he took courses in painting, drawing, and existentialism. He enjoyed the company of the "intellectuals" in those classes and decided "to be one of those." During his army years he was a "closet artist."

In the army he became a crack helicopter pilot. "It was thrilling to be with guys who had flown with John Glenn. In Vietnam I felt like I was in the middle of the history of the world. I couldn't have been more excited with my life. It was thrilling to use my flying skills in the service of my government. I earned my rite of passage into manhood. It was an absurd situation, however, that we were not allowed to shoot unless we were shot at. We followed that order. It occurred to me that we were in Vietnam for strategic, economic reasons."

After leaving the army, Olsen immediately applied to graduate school in art. "Since I had trained in wrestling rather than art, I was required to make artwork to be accepted. As I started working, Vietnam became the subject. I produced thirty-five paintings and got into graduate school."

The skillful etching *Commitment* has the pop art symbols of the sixties—a target, a flag—but also the more personal images of the war experience—barbed wire, helicopters, prisoners at dawn awaiting execution or interrogation. "It's a very felt statement about the sacrifice and commitment of all sides involved not only in the war in Vietnam but in all wars. It's not political. I had Goya's *Garroted Man* in mind." Olsen drew *Tay Ninh* after learning that a friend had been killed in his helicopter in Vietnam. "It's a hell of a way to die. I actually had tears in my eyes as I carved out this picture using a clumsy ebony pencil like a dagger."

Olsen never thought the American involvement in Vietnam was wrong, but he felt an "unspeakable sadness for everyone who died in the war." His attitude has not changed over the years. "No one wants to kill, but the truth is the other guy is there to do the same thing. As time goes on, I have more admiration for all warriors of all states."

Today Olsen treats the war symbolically and abstractly in his art. Yet he knows that, like his hero Ernest Hemingway, he had to be in combat to paint it: "If I had become an artist before I went to Vietnam, I would have been a cubist-trained collegiate."

In Vietnam I felt like I was in the middle of the history of the world. I couldn't have been more excited with my life. It was thrilling to use my flying skills in the service of my government. I earned my rite of passage into manhood.

57. COMMITMENT, *1966,*
intaglio with pouchoir on rag paper, 13 1/2 x 12 inches

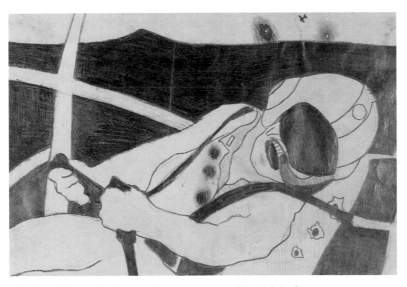

58. TAY NINH, *1967, pencil on rag paper, 12 x 18 inches*

LE TRI DUNG

Napalm and the defoliant Agent Orange were among the most horrendous weapons used by the United States in the war in Vietnam. Though intended to help clear thick jungle growth, Agent Orange has had severe residual effects on both American and Vietnamese soldiers and their children. The painting Le Tri Dung calls *Agent Orange* depicts the tragedy of the herbicide: he shows the ultimate victim, a hideous, humanoid baby, floating in clouds of orange above black, monstrous trees.

LT The American government is aware of the lasting effect of Agent Orange on its veterans and their families but gives little thought to the postwar suffering of countless families in Vietnam. Does this painting speak from your personal experience?

LTD Not mine, but one of my friends had an Agent Orange baby. I was in the area where Agent Orange was used but not for long, so maybe I was not poisoned.

LT Let's talk about your other picture, *After the Bombing at A-Sau*. The marks you make with the pencil are very expressive. Even though they are not specific, they give the feeling of the anxiety of war. Was this your intention?

LTD Yes. This is the Ho Chi Minh Trail in the central highlands. It was bombed when my unit was there.

I am very moved to have met with American veterans. Now we are on the same side communicating through art. The fact that in the past we were enemies and now we are friends makes the exhibition more significant.

LT Were you an army artist?

LTD For the first three years I was in the armored division. I was in the campaign to liberate Saigon. The next four years I was an army painter, recording the movements of my division.

LT When did you start studying art?

LTD When I was four, five, and six years old, I learned a lot from my father, who was a painter. He was one of the first students in the School of Fine Arts in Hanoi, and later became its director. He was also in the art association. When I was eleven, I began seven years of study in a primary and secondary school for art.

LT Do you get a chance to see the work of European artists?

LTD We lack information, but I am lucky to have seen art from foreign countries in Poland. Marc Chagall impressed me very much, and I liked the richness of Salvador Dali.

LT What are you painting now?

LTD Recently, I have been painting the subject of the old people of Vietnam and their traditions. I work most of the time in lacquer.

59. AGENT ORANGE, *1978, painting on silk, 17 1/4 x 22 inches*

60. AFTER THE BOMBING AT A-SAU, *1972,*
charcoal pencil on rice paper,
10 3/4 x 15 1/2 inches

WILLIAM SHORT

*I have returned to Vietnam twice
since my tour of duty ended in
1969. I think I always knew I
would. Like many vets I believed
I left something behind. These
trips have helped me recover some
of what I lost twenty years ago.
They have also brought my war
closer to an end. But until
relations with Vietnam are nor-
malized, I believe the war will
continue for much of America.*

In 1965 William Short was an undergraduate involved in pro-war demonstrations calling for the bombing of Hanoi. He carried a sign that read, "Bomb Ho Chi Minh back to the Stone Age." By 1969 Short was imprisoned in a stockade in Vietnam for refusing to fight. He could find no justification for our involvement in the war. The paranoia about the threat of communism that grew to grotesque proportions in the fifties seemed irrelevant. Short was no longer the naive twenty-year-old who was drafted during the escalation following the Tet Offensive.

"After four months in Vietnam," Short said, "I couldn't understand why I was killing other people and risking my own life. An NCO I admired convinced me to join him in booby-trapping bodies with grenades. Until that time I had avoided looking at dead bodies. I remember noting how heavy the body looked, as if it were glued to the ground. A white bone was exposed where a thumb used to be. I can still see it like a glowing, white ember. It came crashing down on me that I wasn't going to kill any more people."

That resolution led to Short's being court-martialed and imprisoned twice. He was demoted from sergeant to private, stripped of his pay, fined, and given a general discharge. To have given dishonorable discharges to all the rebelling soldiers would have made bad press for an unpopular war.

In his early abstract paintings as well as his recent photographs, Short has mirrored expressionistically the pain and anger he suffered for participating in the war. His documentary photographs, such as those in the exhibition, involve a metaphoric technique of brutalizing the Polaroid negatives as we brutalized Vietnam.

He chose for the show photographs representing the antagonists, *American Embassy, Ho Chi Minh City, 1990* and *Ho Chi Minh's Tomb, 1990*, because of a "strong desire for reconciliation between the two countries." He adds, "In feeling a personal debt to Vietnam, I hope, as an artist, to encourage people of the United States to accept defeat and to enter into a new relationship with the Vietnamese people." Short has himself embarked on that new relationship in two recent trips to Vietnam, during which he developed warm friendships with artists Le Tri Dung, in the North, and Huynh Phuong Dong, in the South.

61. HO CHI MINH'S TOMB, HANOI, 1990,
1990, C-print, 40 x 30 inches

62. AMERICAN EMBASSY, HO CHI MINH CITY, 1990,
1990, C-print, 40 x 30 inches

★

CYNTHIA NORTON

Cynthia Norton grew up in a military family and spent her childhood on military bases. "I loved the military and living on bases where there were 10,000 armed men around me and I was safe. In 1964 we saw all this mobilization of manpower, medical power, and armed power. We didn't care anything about the war. While we were at school, we heard the sound of machine-gun fire and helicopter blades all day long. We never questioned it.

One of the things about the Vietnam War was that women and children were involved. In modern warfare, they are the ones paying the greatest toll. The besieged nation uses the huge loss of women and children as propaganda to get people to fight. The attacking nation demoralizes the target country with these deaths. Both sides profit from these killings. In this way, male power victimizes women and children.

"There was a mock Vietnam village on our beach. It looked just like the real thing and was filled with bombed-out airplane parts. We used to sneak in there at night. In daytime, there would be mock attacks. It was an eerie feeling to imagine what it would be like in battle. It was a kind of envy. I looked at the war strictly as a man's thing. I found myself resenting the fact that I couldn't participate.

"The Vietnam War radically changed my mind. My friends were going to Vietnam and getting killed. My sister's boyfriend was killed at age nineteen. The first painting I ever did about the war was inspired by his death. My father thought it was something to be proud of. I thought that attitude was barbaric.

"I worked with the image of the Vietnam village for a long time. I literally tried to build it with bales of straw. All during the seventies I was making these horrible sculptures. I couldn't seem to get the images I was after. In 1981 I went from sculpture to painting, and 'bam' it happened. The images were in the paint. I started using altar shapes because I wanted to make an American icon. I wanted it to be very clear that war has been glorified in our culture as a rite of passage into manhood.

"One of the things about the Vietnam War, as revealed in news photographs, was that women and children were involved. In modern warfare they are the ones paying the greatest toll. The besieged nation uses the huge loss of women and children as propaganda to get people to fight. The attacking nation demoralizes the target country with these deaths. Both sides profit from these killings. In this way, male power victimizes women and children.

"As a woman, I am especially pleased to be in this show. In *Red Halo* there's a beautiful pastoral setting surrounded by helicopters. Are they there for protection or destruction? It's a painting of opposites—in the color and in the idea of life versus death. *There Is Nothing Too Small* is sarcastic. It's about God, the bullet. Some people don't get it and think it's pro-war. It seems perfectly clear to me, especially with the altar shape, that it's the idolization of war."

63. RED HALOS, *1986,*
acrylic on paper, 51 x 41 inches

64. THERE IS NOTHING TOO SMALL, *1984,*
acrylic and gold leaf on paper, 51 x 41 inches

★

RUDOLF BARANIK

Rudolf Baranik is an abstract painter with soul. Using warm and cool tones of black and white, his work ranges from touching and lyrical to moody and spare. A series of paintings of white writing on black is very affecting. It is visual verse that looks both contemporary and ancient, like hieroglyphic tablets. Baranik explains, "I write with oil stick on a very matte black surface. They're not just marks. They're real words. They're quotations from Eliot and Rilke and letters to our son. I'm not interested in its readability. It's not even readable to me. Basically, I know what is there, but I don't know where."

I'm glad veterans are involved, because all through the years of the antiwar movement, we never had any antagonism toward the American soldiers. I understood that for many it was an infuriating thing they had to do.

It would seem there would be no place for political and figurative art in Baranik's aesthetic. A photograph, however, of a victim of napalm triggered the large series of paintings and collages called *Napalm Elegy*. "It entered and accommodated itself to my work because of its silence. The photograph is a whole, seated figure that looks like a George Segal sculpture, like a calcified, white image from Pompeii. It was the most powerful photograph I had seen come out of Vietnam. It wasn't gory. We were used to that. It was contained and powerful, an icon of suffering."

Eliminating the hospital room in the background of the photograph, Baranik made a poster that is chilling to the core. "I've often thought that this boy or girl—who could tell which?—may be alive today, just as that little Vietnamese girl running naked in that famous photograph. I have been told she studied medicine and was in Cuba." Another work, *Attica, Vietnam*, is a collage of two photographs, one of the napalmed head and the other of the killing of black prisoners at Attica. It is a kind of quiet nightmare journalism of victimization and abuse.

Baranik compares the perceptions of Vietnam in wartime to those in the present. "During the war, we artists were involved in the movement against the war. We thought of Vietnam as almost a holy place—this very poor nation resisting us. The students were chanting, 'Ho Ho Ho Chi Minh, Vietnam is going to win.' Now, Vietnam is an ordinary, Third World, communist country. It is wonderful that we are joined in this exhibition.

"I want to say something about the Americans in this show. I'm glad veterans are involved, because all through the years of the antiwar movement, we never had any antagonism toward the American soldiers. I understood that for many it was an infuriating thing they had to do."

65. Napalm Elegy G6, *1971,*
mixed media, 19 x 23 inches

66. Napalm Elegy G5, *1971,*
mixed media, 25 1/2 x 27 3/4 inches

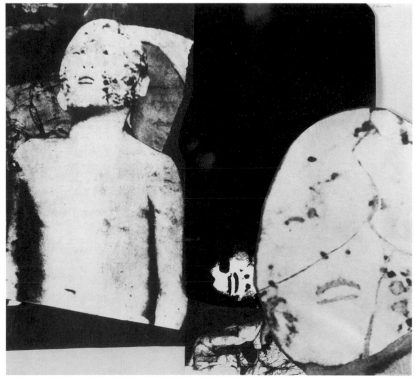

★

While in graduate school Kate Collie met a Vietnam veteran, Steve Piscitelli, who became the inspiration for her paintings on the war. He had heard that she was working on ceramic sculptures and paintings on the themes of violence, aggression, and domination.

"He just showed up with a sculpture of a point man under his arm. He explained that a point man was the first in line to look for mines and ambushes. He told me about his experiences as a point man in the infantry, about fighting hand to hand, and other gruesome things.

"It was a charmed period for both of us. He needed someone to talk to who would listen without judging him. I needed real information about the war to process in my work.

Steve trusted me enough to tell me things that had been buried inside him for years. The more he told me, the more I felt the need to turn the sorrow and confusion I felt into pictures. I tried to encapsulate Steve's pain so other people could see it too, how it was for teenage men who fought a gruesome, thankless war.

"For two years he talked to me, suggested books to read, and introduced me to other veterans. I tried to understand post-traumatic stress syndrome. I was shocked to the core to learn that more veterans had committed suicide than were killed in the war. I did a lot of research, and after a couple of years started making paintings about that issue.

"The first paintings on the Vietnam War were like the ones in this exhibition. I did a series of twenty very small, understated symbolic still lifes that were based on Steve's stories. I called them *Poems*. *By a Thread* is about the tenuousness of life. A little object is hanging by a thread that could break but hasn't. The wishbone represents two opposites, hope and death. *Steve's Mementos* shows his daily dosage of prescription medication: painkillers, tranquilizers, and antipsychotics. *60,000 Suicides* consists of two works, one with text. I wanted the screw eye to look like a question mark and also to be a *screw*. In the background is the Vietnam Service Medal. In the foreground is a razor blade for slitting one's wrist.

"I did a series of seven large canvases telling Steve's story. They're mainly interiors. There's Steve in his room surrounded by his sculpture. Another is of him receiving the Purple Heart in a Quonset hut hospital in Da Nang.

"I tried, in making the Vietnam paintings, to do something for the veterans. I wanted to elucidate the issues to help people understand what it was to fight the war. After most of the paintings were finished, I realized that was not the whole story. I was also painting about myself and my experiences, my big disillusionments. It helped me understand the emotional and psychological situations in my life that were so clearly delineated in the Vietnam veteran, especially Steve."

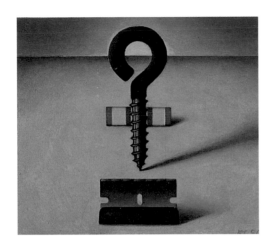

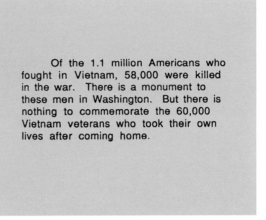

Of the 1.1 million Americans who fought in Vietnam, 58,000 were killed in the war. There is a monument to these men in Washington. But there is nothing to commemorate the 60,000 Vietnam veterans who took their own lives after coming home.

67. 60,000 SUICIDES, *1986, oil on masonite, with separate text on paper, 5 1/2 x 6 inches*

68. BY A THREAD, *1986,*
oil on masonite, 5 1/2 x 6 inches

69. STEVE'S MEMENTOS, *1987,*
oil on paper, 4 1/4 x 5 3/8 inches

★

RICK DROZ

Every year Rick Droz, a former Marine and member of a group called Peace for Action, visits high-school classes to speak to students about the Vietnam War. His motive is clear: he wants "to tell them what I wasn't told about Vietnam" so that they will better understand issues of war and peace.

In some ways my life revolves around my experience in Vietnam. It was a profound, ultimately good experience, but I shudder to say it because I was personally responsible for making the lives of many Vietnamese miserable, intolerable. Am I a better person for this? That is a question I expect to try to answer for the rest of my life. I witnessed the most horrific acts known to mankind, I am a survivor of an atrocity, and I have no choice but to educate others.

RD Two weeks after I got there, I knew damn well we shouldn't be there. Not one person I was with knew why we were there and could justify killing other human beings. After a week in heavy combat I knew enough about my so-called enemy to have an enormous amount of respect for him. He was willing to die for what he was fighting for. I didn't meet one American willing to die for what we were fighting for if, indeed, he knew what that was.

LT You saw a lot of combat, didn't you?

RD Yes, I did. I was wounded and had several amputations to my right leg starting with my toes and working up to above the knee. I spent a month in Vietnam in very critical condition. Eventually, I stayed seven months in a California hospital. It was a blessing in disguise. It gave me the time I needed to regain some of my social composure. My family and friends took good care of me, but nobody wanted to talk about the war. I had no place to verbalize my anger and frustration. Even now, there isn't a day that goes by that I don't think of the atrocities I did.

LT How did you get into photography, and has it served as an outlet for you?

RD I was working as a mechanic on a top-secret project for an aerospace company. I quit after two weeks upon learning what the spacecraft actually did. I thought about what I'd like to do. It was photography. It's a powerful way to communicate. I found I could use a camera very well and had artistic ability. It's a sensitive, almost sensual way to express myself.

LT What led you to do these moving photographs?

RD I went to the Veterans Administration Hospital in San Francisco to get a state-of-the-art leg. I met with a board of therapists, prosthetists, and doctors. Behind them was a huge glass case containing the most gruesome artificial arms, legs, feet, and hands. They looked like weapons—mortar tubes and rocket launchers. Photographic images started spinning in my head. The idea was to combine the limbs with the real weapons. To get the weapons, I had to gain the trust of veterans who possessed them. Some of the men, for protection, lived like hermits. It took over a year, and I made only four photographs.

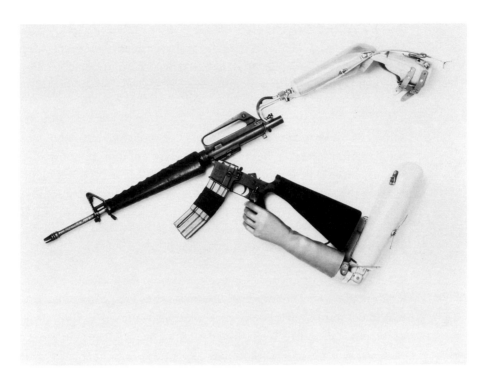

70. WOUNDED CHILDREN #16, *1988, photograph, 11 x 14 inches*

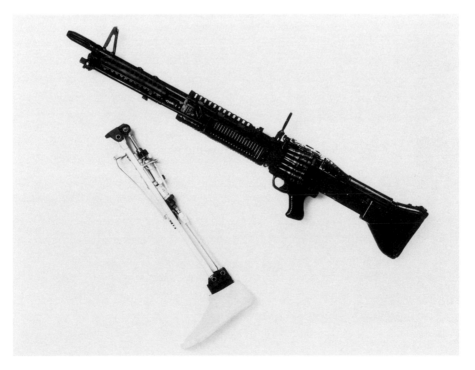

71. WOUNDED CHILDREN #60, *1988, photograph, 11 x 14 inches*

TRAN VIET SON

Tran Viet Son, the current president of the Fine Arts Department of the Ministry of Culture, is an extraordinary draftsman. As an army artist during the war, he drew many images of American prisoners and their accoutrements. These drawings are visual reportage capturing the essential nature of a sleeping GI or the look of a well-used boot.

LT Why did you draw these prisoners?

Many American prisoners told me and my friends that their knowledge of Vietnam had changed. At first they thought the Vietnamese people just fought and fought, and that there were no people like doctors, painters, and poets. Now their perceptions changed.

TVS I considered our fighters heroes and heroines. In order to show the results of their bravery, I had to draw the prisoners. As army artists, we worked like journalists and photographers. We went to the areas to make contact and then get into our work. These drawings show the daily activities of the prisoners—sleeping, talking together. In one the leader from the National Liberation Front explains the clemency policy.

LT There's a lot of documentation about the prisoners in these drawings. Where did you get this information?

TVS The soldier in charge of the prisoners gave me this information, and some of them I interviewed myself.

LT What, if anything, did the Americans say about their experience?

TVS Many American prisoners told me and my friends that their knowledge of Vietnam had changed. At first they thought the Vietnamese people just fought and fought, and that there were no people like doctors, painters, and poets. Now their perceptions changed.

LT You are an accomplished draftsman. Where did you get your training?

TVS I was very interested in art as a child. I watched many films showing how to paint by Huan Tu Dis Nai, one of our artists. When I was a schoolboy, I tried my best to make good drawings. Then in 1958 I was appointed by the army to take a course in fine art. I studied for seven years at the School of Fine Arts in Hanoi. After the war I studied from 1975 to 1979 in the German Democratic Republic. From 1982 to 1983 I was the vice-director of the School of Fine Arts in Hanoi.

LT Does your job at the Ministry of Culture allow you time for your own work?

TVS About fifty percent of the time. I wish to have one hundred percent. If this position is given to someone else, I can spend all of my time painting.

72. SKETCH OF AMERICAN SOLDIERS, *1968, ink on paper, 7 x 10 1/4 inches*

74. SKETCH AT THE BATTLE, *1968,*
ink on paper, 7 1/2 x 10 1/2 inches

73. SKETCH OF AMERICAN ARMY UNIFORM,
1968, ink and pencil on paper, 10 1/4 x 7 inches

D O   H I E N

Do Hien has been a leader of anti-aircraft troops, an army artist and journalist, and now a coordinator of the Pioneer House for young boys, where he also teaches drawing. Among the works of the Vietnamese artists, his collage painting is unique. Its use of found materials relates more to the mixed-media work of New York artists. Do Hien, however, has had no exposure to contemporary American art, though he enjoys the work of Picasso, Gauguin, and Modigliani. He chose his materials with the sole intention of moving his viewers. He considers his work to be in line with the traditional Vietnamese aesthetic.

LT In Vietnam there is a traditional and popular use of paper in the decorative arts for lanterns, masks, and such things. Do you feel there is a connection to this custom in your work?

DH Yes, the traditional uses of paper have a real place in my work. I use paper instead of paint when the paper has stronger color. It is also smoother.

LT What do you call this painting?

DH *The Anniversary of the National Defense War.* It is a traditional painting of the people of Vietnam. The materials carry with them the Vietnamese characteristics. My intention was to speak with the color. The strong yellow is to encourage the people to enjoy peace.

The picture contains three subjects: one is the image of the anti-aircraft fighter; the second one with the dove is the victory after 1975; the third is the festival dealing with women and children enjoying the peace. It shows the gloriousness of the yellow fruit. Traditionally, Vietnamese people use fine fruit for the festival as an offering to the souls of the people who have died.

LT Please talk about *Alien at Quang Binh.*

DH Immediately after the downing of a United States aircraft by my unit, I made this painting. It shows the helmet of the pilot and the paper he carried with him, which said in many languages "Do not be afraid. I am your friend."

The mother and child were my own inspiration. I watched the pilot die. He held a handkerchief that showed he was in love. Just as I was affected by the sacrifices of the Vietnamese in war, I was moved by the sacrifice on this American's part.

I hope to make drawings of the war from memory. There was an exhibition in Hanoi on the subject of the soldiers on the Ho Chi Minh Trail. I made an oil painting for it that was highly appreciated. This encouraged me to think of the past, and I wish to draw the war.

75. ALIEN AT QUANG BINH, *1971,*
ink on paper, 11 1/2 x 6 1/2 inches

76. THE ANNIVERSARY OF THE NATIONAL DEFENSE WAR,
1989, collage and paint on paper, 18 3/4 x 33 1/2 inches

TRAN KHANH CHUONG

Tran Khanh Chuong has a strong background in ceramics. He studied at the School of Industrial Arts in Hanoi and in China and has also worked at the ceramic factory in Hai Sung. The works in the exhibition, however, are plastercuts. Khanh Chuong makes very fine prints with this technique and recently won an award at the International Graphic Art Exhibition in Berlin. He has participated in exhibitions in Poland, Bulgaria, France, and the Soviet Union and this year held an acclaimed one-man exhibition in Paris. Khanh Chuong's work is, in his words, "a combination of the national style and modern art."

LT Plastercut is a new medium to me. Can you tell me how you make your prints?

I hope that the American people will understand the Vietnamese people through our art. The Vietnamese people love peace and friendship between nations.

TKC In Vietnam our tradition of woodcuts is very famous. We also import methods like stone rubbings and etching from other countries. We don't have a tradition of plaster carving. We thought of this method because wood for art is very rare, and plaster is available and cheap. I have used this method since 1978.

First, I pour plaster into a flat mold. Then I make a drawing and cut the image. Next, I use a substance that seals the plaster but holds the ink. The paint is tempera. I use many colors, but I have one plastercut. I print each color separately on the black paper. I use my hand for pressure to print.

LT Tell me about the content of *Giong*.

TKC It is the story of the little boy hero Giong, who magically grows up very quickly because of the invasion of Vietnam by China. He becomes a hero when he pushes out the aggressors. His weapon is a bamboo tree. Many artists in Vietnam use this story to say something about the Giong hero. In my imagination, he is a little boy without clothing who goes to the frontier with the encouragement of the flowers and the birds. The horse is made of iron and breathes fire like a dragon. Any Vietnamese in your country can tell you this story.

LT Now, tell me about *The Happy Day of Liberation*.

TKC It recalls October 10, 1954, and the liberation from the French. It shows the Long Son Market, where the Vietnamese soldiers forced the French to withdraw.

LT You were about eleven years old at the time of the liberation. Did you witness it?

TKC No, but I saw a documentary film on it. The atmosphere in Hanoi in 1954 was very exciting. It was the same in 1975 in both Hanoi and Ho Chi Minh City. I was a soldier at that time. I celebrated and drank too much wine.

77. THE HAPPY DAY OF LIBERATION, *1986,*
plastercut on black rice paper, 15 1/4 x 15 1/2 inches

78. GIONG, *1982,*
plastercut on black rice paper, 16 x 16 inches

★

WENDY V. WATRISS

As a young girl growing up in Europe in the fifties, Wendy Watriss saw the poverty and suffering that followed World War II. In her work as a photographer and documentary filmmaker, she has gravitated to themes of need and injustice as well as to sociological and political subjects. She became interested in the Vietnam War in 1980.

Since 1982, when the Vietnam Veterans Memorial opened, I've been back many times. I find the people's response to the memorial and to each other very moving. It shows again that war doesn't end when the combat is over.

WVW There hadn't been any still documentation of the Agent Orange story. It took a year and a half to cover this subject. Halfway through, I took some photographs to *Life* magazine, which paid for the balance of the work and published the story. With that body of photographs, I have been able to work with veterans' groups in Texas, where I now live, to get legislation passed to establish a research program for health problems and an advocacy platform for future research.

LT In orphanages in Vietnam we saw the effects of Agent Orange on children.

WVW After the photographs were published, one of the first things I did was to find the work of three photographers—Welsh, English, and Japanese—who had documented the effects of Agent Orange. I laminated the work so it could be tacked up anywhere, in country courthouses, medical teaching institutions, libraries, and meeting places for veterans' groups. Since 1983 the exhibition has been around the country many times. It's very powerful, showing the effects of dioxin on American, Vietnamese, and Australian servicemen and also on English farm workers.

LT One of your photographs in this show is of a veteran and his family.

WVW Yes, Dan Loney had many symptoms related to toxic chemical exposure—numbness, nausea, and headaches. I spent the morning and afternoon photographing the family. The wife had had several miscarriages. The daughter was born with an arm that ends below her shoulder. She's very beautiful.

The other photograph is of Daniel Salmon, who had made a career in the Air Force as an electrician. He served two tours in Vietnam, where he helped clear land for airstrips. They used a defoliant, and he was exposed repeatedly. Several years later he developed nausea, headaches, intestinal problems, and sores. Some of his fingers were amputated and then both legs. He died in 1984. After leaving the Air Force, he couldn't, for a long time, get social security disability or medical benefits. His death report does say his health problems could have resulted from Agent Orange.

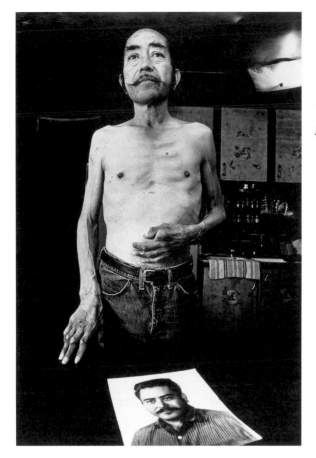

79. Daniel Salmon, *1983,*
photograph, 16 1/2 x 11 inches

80. Barbara Loney, *1981,*
photograph, 11 x 16 1/2 inches

After many years of living and working in Paris, Nancy Spero and her husband, Leon Golub, returned to the United States in 1964. Back on her own turf and with the constant barrage of media coverage, Spero became fully aware of the reality of the Vietnam War and felt the need to respond to it in her work. It was an issue closely related to the victimization of women, which would become a deep concern and the focus of future work.

"Somehow the horror of it got to me. I had three small sons, and I didn't like what was happening. In Europe I had been doing a series of dark paintings of lovers. I decided there would be a big change in my work. I was just appalled at the carnage and very disappointed that we were acting like any other colonialist empire, taking over and judging other nations. The work would be about violence, collusion, and power.

I started to think about how to address the war. I would do it in such a way as to show the collusion of sex and power, and I would do it in such a way as to shock the viewer. I wanted it to be obscene, because the war was obscene.

"I started to think about how to address the war. I would do it in such a way as to show the collusion of sex and power, and I would do it in such a way as to shock the viewer. It took me a year to figure out the iconography of the bomb. The column of the bomb would be the body of a man. They were male bombs, so it was phallic power. The resulting clouds would be angry heads spewing out poison on the victims. I wanted it to be obscene, because the war was obscene.

"After nine months of doing the bomb, I concluded that the real symbol of the Vietnam War was the helicopter. I anthropomorphized the helicopter just as I did the bomb. Again, these were male helicopters with blades like penises. It was male power destructively thrashing about. Then, I thought, 'What would the peasants think of these gunships coming down and bombing and napalming?' So, I turned the helicopters into prehistoric, pterodactyl-like creatures. Perhaps the peasants would think of them as creatures of evil, as I did.

"In the lithograph in the exhibition, *Thou Shalt Not Kill*, a Vietnamese woman flees from danger with her baby. They are the true victims of war. The other piece is a collage. It's a photostat of a helicopter gunship. A cord hangs from it, from which I suspended a Christ figure. Then I printed PEACE with stencils in manifesto-like fashion.

"America lost a lot of credibility talking about *our* generosity, *our* largess, *our* fairness, when in reality we were just like the other rapacious countries. It was such a great disappointment. We all saw what was happening, but it took such a long time for it to stop. And just look how we're continuing with this interference in other parts of the world!"

81. Peace, *1968, hand-printed collage and Xerox collage on paper, 19 x 24 inches*

82. Thou Shalt Not Kill, *1987,*
lithograph and letterpress on rag paper, 23 1/2 x 17 3/4 inches

CHECKLIST

1, 2   Nguyen Tho Tuong
b. 1953, Nai Ding Province, Vietnam
School of Fine Arts, Hanoi

3, 4   Michael Aschenbrenner
b. 1949, Los Angeles, California
MFA, University of Minnesota, Minneapolis
Resides in New York City

5, 6   Huynh Phuong Dong
b. 1925, Saigon, Vietnam
School of Practical Art, Saigon
School of Fine Arts, Hanoi

7, 8   Leon Golub
b. 1922, Chicago, Illinois
MFA, School of the Art Institute of Chicago
Resides in New York City

9, 10   John Plunkett
b. 1948, Oceanside, Long Island, New York
BFA, School of the Visual Arts, New York
MFA, Rhode Island School of Design
Resides in Mt. Kisco, New York

11, 12   Cliff Joseph
b. 1932, Panama
BFA, Pratt Institute
MFA, Pratt Institute
Resides in New York City

13–16   Tran Trung Tin
b. 1933, Saigon, Vietnam

17, 18   Ngan Chai
b. 1954, Nguy Tinh Province, Vietnam
School of Fine Arts, Hanoi

19   Nguyen The Minh
b. 1937, Hanoi, Vietnam
School of Fine Arts, Hanoi

20, 21   Nguyen Nghia Duyen
b. 1943, Dong Ho, Vietnam

22, 23   Pham Nguyen Hung
b. 1942, Hai Phong, Vietnam
School of Fine Arts, Hanoi

24, 25   C. David Thomas
b. 1946, Portland, Maine
MFA, Rhode Island School of Design
Resides in Newton Centre, Massachusetts

26, 27   Tin Ly
b. 1953, Saigon, Vietnam
BMus., Indiana University, Bloomington
Resides in Fort Lauderdale, Florida

28, 29   James R. Cannata
b. 1949, East Liverpool, Ohio
BA, Metropolitan State College, Denver
MFA, Florida State University, Tallahassee
Resides in Denver, Colorado

30, 31   David Schirm
b. 1945, Pittsburgh, Pennsylvania
MFA, Indiana University, Bloomington
Resides in Batavia, New York

32, 33   May Stevens
b. 1924, Boston, Massachusetts
BFA, Massachusetts College of Art
Resides in New York City

34   David Smith
b. 1950, Portland, Oregon
BFA, Pomona College
Resides in New York City

35, 36   Vu Giang Huong
b. 1930, Hanoi, Vietnam
School of Fine Arts, Hanoi

37, 38   Nguyen The Huu
b. 1946, Quan Bin Province, Vietnam
School of Fine Arts, Hanoi

39, 40   Trinh Kim Vinh
b. 1932, Vietnam
School of Fine Arts, Hanoi
Dresden University, East Germany

41, 42   Tran Te
b. 1936, Tang Hua Province, Vietnam
School of Fine Arts, Hanoi

43, 44 Arnold Trachtman
b. 1930, Lynn, Massachusetts
MFA, School of the Art Institute of Chicago
Resides in Cambridge, Massachusetts

45, 46 Bui Tan Hung
b. 1932, Kung Ta, Vietnam
School of Fine Arts, Hanoi

47, 48 Quach Van Phong
b. 1938, Khu Lam, Vietnam
School of Fine Arts, Hanoi

49, 50 Nguyen Minh Dinh
b. 1940, Singha, Vietnam
School of Industrial Arts, Hanoi

51, 52 Benny Andrews
b. 1930, Madison, Georgia
BFA, School of the Art Institute of Chicago
Resides in New York City

53, 54 Tran Thanh Lam
b. 1949, Hue, Vietnam
School of Fine Arts, Hanoi
School of Fine Arts, Ho Chi Minh City

55, 56 Nguyen Tuan Khanh (Rung)
b. 1941, Phnom Penh, Cambodia
School of Fine Arts, Hue

57, 58 Richard J. Olsen
b. 1935, Milwaukee, Wisconsin
BA, University of Wisconsin, Madison
MFA, University of Wisconsin, Madison
Resides in Athens, Georgia

59, 60 Le Tri Dung
b. 1949, Hanoi, Vietnam
School of Fine Arts, Hanoi

61, 62 William Short
b. 1947, Cincinnati, Ohio
BFA, Antioch College
MFA, University of Southern California
Resides in Cambridge, Massachusetts

63, 64 Cynthia Norton
b. 1950, Newport, Rhode Island
BFA, University of Texas, Austin
Resides in Lyons, Pennsylvania

65, 66 Rudolf Baranik
b. 1920, Lithuania
School of the Art Institute of Chicago
Art Students League of New York
Resides in New York City

67–69 Kate Collie
b. 1954, Cambridge, England
BA, State University of New York, Binghamton
MFA, University of Massachusetts, Amherst
Resides in Charlotte, North Carolina

70, 71 Rick Droz
b. 1949, Pasadena, California
BA, Brooks Institute, Santa Barbara
Resides in Fort Brag, California

72–74 Tran Viet Son
b. 1935, Hanoi, Vietnam
School of Fine Arts, Hanoi

75, 76 Do Hien
b. 1943, Hanoi, Vietnam
School of Fine Arts, Vietnam

77, 78 Tran Khanh Chuong
b. 1943, Hanoi, Vietnam
School of Industrial Arts, Hanoi

79, 80 Wendy V. Watriss
b. 1944, San Francisco, California
BA, New York University
Resides in Houston, Texas

81, 82 Nancy Spero
b. 1926, Cleveland, Ohio
BFA, School of the Art Institute of Chicago
Resides in New York City